Baseball and Memory

Baseball and Memory

Winning, Losing, and the
Remembrance of Things Past

Lee Congdon

ST. AUGUSTINE'S PRESS
South Bend, Indiana

Manufactured in the United States of America

1 2 3 4 5 6   16 15 14 13 12 11

Library of Congress Cataloging in Publication Data
Congdon, Lee, 1939–
Baseball and memory : winning, losing, and
the remembrance of things past / Lee Congdon.
p. cm.
Includes bibliographical references and index.
ISBN 978-1-58731-063-8 (hardback)
1. Baseball – United States – History. 2. Baseball – Social
aspects – United States. 3. Memory. I. Title.
GV863.A1C5937 2011
796.3570973 – dc22   2011009658

∞ The paper used in this publication meets the minimum requirements of the American National Standard for Information Sciences – Permanence of Paper for Printed Materials, ANSI Z39.48-1984.

ST. AUGUSTINE'S PRESS
www.staugustine.net

To Kenneth Dawson

Baseball and memory come together so naturally.
– Roger Angell

Memory is like baseball.
– Buck O'Neil

The deep eros of memory that separates
baseball from other sports.
– Don DeLillo

Contents

Preface

THIS IS A HISTORICAL AND PHILOSOPHICAL REFLECTION ON A GAME AND the ways in which it spurs memory. We live in a time in which memory of the past is fading. Students at every grade level across the land seem to suffer from a form of amnesia, and their mentors no longer instill in them the discipline of memorization—of poems, speeches, and plays. Exercises of that kind are thought to be beneath them. What they and many of their elders do remember, or think they remember, is often highly selective. "I continue to be troubled," the philosopher Paul Ricoeur wrote, "by the unsettling spectacle offered by an excess of memory here, and an excess of forgetting elsewhere." We are, for example, endlessly reminded of Nazi crimes, but very rarely of those committed by Communists. Laudatory books on the 1960s proliferate, while those on the 1950s are rare and almost uniformly critical.

Baseball can, and does, serve as an important corrective, for as Roger Angell, one of the finest of baseball writers, has observed: "Baseball and memory come together so naturally." When we remember important events and players from the game's past, we discover that they are inextricably intertwined with particular eras in the nation's history: Babe Ruth and the Jazz Age, Joe DiMaggio and the country at war, Willie Mays and the 1950s. In often revelatory ways, those eras come alive again and as a result we gain greater self-knowledge—or, better said, greater self-understanding. Moreover, we begin to revive a sense of community.

In what follows, I have remembered some of baseball's greatest figures and moments. And I have attempted to show how memory flows naturally from some of baseball's most storied victories, and some of its most stunning losses, to the larger world of an era. Finally, I have focused primarily on the decade of the 1950s because I believe it to have been baseball's golden age—and a far better time in America than many have been taught to think. It was a time of cultural (high and popular) seriousness and achievement, the like of which we have not seen since. I endeavor too to show how most of the charges leveled at the decade are demonstrably false and misleading. Like the story of baseball, I conclude, the story of America since the 1950s has been one of decline. Remembering baseball, and especially remembering baseball in the 1950s, can provide hope that that decline might yet be reversed.

Acknowledgments

THIS BOOK HAS BEEN IN THE MAKING SINCE THE DAY IN 1948 THAT MY father took me to Wrigley Field for the first time. My greatest debt is to him and to my mother, who was also an avid Cub fan. For some reason, she took a particular liking to Roy Smalley, a career .232 hitter as a Cub. After reading that the modestly talented shortstop was striving to increase his power at the plate by drinking milk shakes, she assured her friends that he would soon take his rightful place among the game's élite. I wish she and my father had lived to read this book.

Growing up in the suburbs of Chicago, most of my friends were, and still are, Cub fans. Our continued friendship has much to do with our shared baseball memories and inextinguishable hope that we may one day attend a World Series game in the "Friendly Confines."

Special thanks are due to my agent, Jeremy Beer, who offered me valuable editorial and substantive suggestions, and gave me my subtitle. I am grateful to Bruce Fingerhut, President of St. Augustine's Press, for his interest in my work, professional counsel, and shared love of the game. John Horne, a photo archivist at the Hall of Fame, gave generously of his time in order to present me with the many excellent photographs from which I made the selections included in the book. For so many things—having little to do with baseball—I am indebted to my wife Carol, my son Mitchell, my daughter Colleen, and my daughter-in-law Jennifer. It is impossible to imagine life without them.

I have dedicated this book to a man who has been more like a brother than a friend since the day in 1962 that we met in the orderly room at the Army Language School in Monterey, California. In his youth, he was a hard-throwing right-hander, and I have no doubt that he could still strike terror in the hearts of hitters.

Harrisonburg, Virginia
January 11, 2011

Introduction

"WHERE WERE YOU WHEN YOU HEARD THAT THE JAPANESE HAD attacked Pearl Harbor?" To members of my parents' generation that question was full of meaning not only because it bound them to their country and countrymen as never before, but because it caused them to think back upon their lives. To those of my generation, born between 1935 and 1945, the corresponding question was "where were you when you learned that President Kennedy had been shot in Dallas?" For a younger generation it undoubtedly is "where were you the morning of September 11, 2001?" It may seem strange to the latter generation—for the members of which baseball is no longer the national pastime—that men and women of a certain age became more self-aware when asked where they were when Bobby Thomson hit "the shot heard round the world"—the home run that, on October 3, 1951, brought a sudden and stunning end to the most dramatic pennant race in baseball history.

Thomson's home run was far less important than acts of war or a presidential assassination, and yet the novelist Don DeLillo was serious when he asked: "Isn't it possible that this mid-century moment enters the skin more lastingly than the vast shaping strategies of eminent leaders, generals steely in their sunglasses?" In part, no doubt, the lasting impact of Thomson's round-tripper has something to do with the fact that he hit it in New York, the great cultural center that was, at the time, the unchallenged capital of the baseball world. In the decade extending from 1947 to 1957, the three New York teams—Yankees, Giants, and Dodgers—dominated the game. Because they played in the same

1

league, the Giant–Dodger rivalry was especially intense, and the 1951 contest particularly riveting. That contest can be said to have begun in earnest on June 15 (the trading deadline), when the lowly Chicago Cubs sent their best player, outfielder-third baseman Andy Pafko, and three lesser mortals to Brooklyn in an eight-player deal.

"Handy Andy" had broken in with the Cubs late in 1943; he appeared in 13 games and hit .379. His average dropped to a modest .269 in 1944, but the following year he helped lead the Cubs to the National League championship, batting a solid .298 and knocking in 110 runs. The North Siders lost the World Series to Detroit's Tigers and then began to slide. They finished third in 1946, a year in which Pafko played in only 65 games. Having recovered from injuries, he performed well the following year, but the Cubs still ended up in sixth place. In 1948, the year of my baseball awakening, they finished eighth—last—even though Pafko batted .312, hit 26 home runs, and drove in 101 runs.

Of the 1949 and 1950 Cubs the less said the better, but Pafko continued to excel. He was, however, a bit off his game when the Cubs traded him. To move from a cellar-bound team to a pennant favorite might seem like an answer to prayer, but Wrigley Field casts mysterious spells; Pafko wept. Those were the years before free agency. A player might wear two or three uniforms in the course of his career but not seven or eight—or more. So there was a sense of loyalty, at least on the players' part. Moreover, Pafko was born in Wisconsin, and he and his wife felt at home in the Windy City.

To the Dodgers, however, he dutifully reported. He must have felt a great deal of pressure, for he knew that he had been brought in to ensure a championship. ("Gentlemen, we have just traded for the pennant," a Dodger official said at the time.) He joined a team that has had few equals: Gil Hodges at first base, Jackie Robinson at second, Billy Cox at third, Pee Wee Reese at shortstop, Roy Campanella behind the plate, Duke Snider in center field, Carl Furillo in right. Don Newcombe, Carl Erskine, and Ralph Branca were the mainstays of the pitching staff.

Only Leo Durocher's Giants posed a threat to the talented "Bums." They had rookie sensation Willie Mays in center field and Don Mueller in right; Monte Irvin, like Mays a former Negro Leaguer, patrolled left. At first base was Whitey Lockman, at second the "brat," Eddie Stanky. Alvin Dark, master of the art of hitting behind the runner, was the shortstop. To make room for Mays, Durocher had moved outfielder Thomson to third base. Wes Westrum handled the catching for a pitching staff anchored by Sal "The Barber" Maglie, Larry Jansen, and Jim Hearn.

As good as the Giants were, however, they did not appear to be good enough. By August 11, they had fallen 13 ½ games behind the league-leading Dodgers; but then the charge began. Over their final 44 games, the Giants notched 37 victories, including a sweep of the last seven. While the Giants surged, the Dodgers struggled. They won only 24 of their last 44, and lost six of their last ten. At the end of the regular season, therefore, each team had a record of 96-58. For only the second time in its history, the National League prepared for a playoff series—best of three.

The Giants captured the first game, played at Brooklyn's Ebbets Field, 3-1; the Dodgers took the second, in the Polo Grounds, 10-0. The entire season came down to a final game in the Polo Grounds. Dodger skipper Charlie Dressen sent Newcombe to the mound, while Durocher handed the ball to Maglie. Pafko started in left field and contributed a scratch hit to a Dodger rally that put them ahead 4-1 going into the last of the ninth; the "boys of summer" (as Roger Kahn has called them) needed only three more outs.

Giant fans began to come alive when Alvin Dark led off the inning with a single off Hodges's glove and advanced to third on Mueller's hard-hit single through the spot where Hodges, who had been told by Dressen to hold Dark on, should have been playing. When Monte Irvin fouled out, hope dwindled, but all was not yet lost. Whitey Lockman laced Newcombe's second pitch down the line in left, and by the time Pafko retrieved and fired the ball back to the infield, Dark had scored. Mueller broke his ankle sliding into third; Clint Hartung was inserted as a pinch-runner, and the tying runs were in scoring position when Bobby Thomson walked to the plate.

Dressen removed Newcombe, who was about to collapse from fatigue. Now he had a crucial decision to make. Should he call upon Clem Labine, who had pitched game two, or the more experienced Carl Erskine? In the end, he relied upon pitching coach Clyde Sukeforth's judgment and summoned Ralph Branca, who had served a gopher ball to Thomson in game one of the series. The lanky right-hander—who wore number 13—started Thomson off with a fastball strike on the inside corner. His next pitch was up and in, but Thomson leaned back and connected. Pafko raced to the 17-foot wall in left—and never forgot what he saw. "It was a hard shot, right down the line. I wasn't aware at first that it was going in for a homer. But when it passed over my head, the whole thing became a terrible blur. I had the best view of it of anyone in the house—and wish I hadn't."

The time was 3:58 p.m. on the east coast. Pandemonium ensued. A Brooklyn man taped Giant broadcaster Russ Hodges as he shouted into the microphone: "The Giants win the pennant, the Giants win the pennant, the Giants win the pennant, the Giants win the pennant. . . . I don't believe it, I don't believe it, I do not believe it." Probably the most famous call in history.

The young DeLillo, a Yankee fan, did not hear Hodges's call because he was sitting in a dentist's chair. In 1991, on the game's fortieth anniversary, he happened upon a newspaper story that brought that moment back to him. When, out of curiosity, he looked up the October 4, 1951, edition of the *New York Times*, he was struck by the juxtaposition of the two leading headlines: "Giants Capture Pennant, Beating Dodgers 5-4 on Thomson's 3-Run Homer" and "Soviet's Second Atom Blast in 2 Years Revealed by U.S.; Details Are Kept a Secret." At that moment, he felt the power of history as never before.

It was not an altogether satisfying feeling. History, he feared, set limits to the creative imagination. The novelist had therefore to fight back—with language as his weapon of choice. "Language," DeLillo has written, "can be a form of counterhistory"; it can transform the past. It can make it possible for us to experience historical events more fully and discover hidden truths about historical figures—and ultimately about ourselves. In what was to serve as a prologue to *Underworld*, a novel about America in the second half of the twentieth century, DeLillo retold the story of Thomson's home run and imagined the fate of the ball—never in fact recovered—as it migrated from one possessor to another; on each person, the ball seems to produce a strange effect.

For good reason. Unlike other balls, that one had been touched by history in a special way. To hold it was to summon memories, to rescue a past from oblivion. You relived that past, or rather you *lived* it, for it pervaded your existence in the here and now. The past had been transmuted from the base metal of the transitory into the gold of the eternal. That is why memory is not merely a vehicle of nostalgia but a fundamental ingredient in a richer and more intensely lived life.

Recognizing the prologue to *Underworld* as a triumph of the art of reliving, DeLillo's publisher reissued it as a novella bearing the title *Pafko at the Wall*. Because DeLillo has a fine ear for the way people speak, the words he gave to Frank Sinatra, Jackie Gleason, Toots Shor, and J. Edgar Hoover—all of whom watched the game from Durocher's box—possess a historically specific texture. In brilliant fashion, too, DeLillo summoned the midcentury to life by imagining what was printed on the scraps of newspapers and magazines that fans showered on Pafko and those sitting in the lower boxes: ads for products such as Borden's pasteurized processed cheese, Packards, and RCA Victor. A nightclub photo from *Life* magazine lands near Sinatra. It is of him and screen goddess Ava Gardner, soon to be his wife.

A magazine reproduction of the Flemish master Pieter Bruegel the Elder's nightmarish *Triumph of Death* (1562) falls on Hoover's shoulder, and his fascination with it served as DeLillo's way of exposing the FBI director's inner demons and preoccupation with communism and the threat of nuclear war. Hoover has already been informed that the Soviet Union had tested the bomb for a second time. In this way, DeLillo brought the Cold War into his portrait of the American midcentury. And yet it was still the game as an object of endless fascination—a headline in the *New York Times* as large as that devoted to the Soviet test—that he sought to understand. Much of the fascination, DeLillo thought, derives from our longing to feel linked to others through time. He wrote of "the fans' intimate wish to be connected to the event." In that way they attained a kind of immortality; they became part of something that would be remembered long after they themselves are forgotten.

But the fans also wished to be connected to other people, to feel themselves members of a community. DeLillo described the hours after the game in this way: "All over the city people are coming out of their houses. This is the nature of Thomson's homer. It makes people want to be in the streets, joined with others, telling others what has happened, those few who haven't heard—comparing faces and states of mind." Later, even decades later, they remain bound to others by a shared memory.

This is all true, but there is something more, something DeLillo hinted at when he described Thomson leaping around the bases after the ball crashed into the lower deck in left: "He is forever Bobby now, a romping boy lost to time." The home run will live forever in our collective memory, handed down from generation to generation. In that way, like all great moments in the game's history, it strengthens the bonds that link us not only to others of our time but to our fathers, forefathers, and children.

It is a truism of social commentary that many in America and the Western world generally have lost any thick sense of community. They have lost all sense of those vital links that make strong families and nations, and instead live as mere aggregates of isolated individuals whose only relationship to others is that dictated by self-interest or prescribed by law. Theorists and social therapists have proposed all manner of projects, many of them utopian, to quicken that atrophied sense. But success will continue to elude us unless we first rebuild unity across time by remembering and respecting the past and those who lived in it. Society, Edmund Burke once wrote, is "a partnership not only between those who are living, but between those who are living, those who are dead, and those who are to be born."

Historical memory is necessary not only to the reconstruction of community, but to the preservation of our individual selfhood. In the words of Robert Penn Warren, "any true self is not only the result of a vital relation with a community but is also a development in time, and if there is no past there can be no self." An amnesiac is still a human being, but not fully a person, a self. For what is the self? "It is," the Czech writer Milan Kundera has observed, "the sum of everything we remember. Thus, what terrifies us about death is not the loss of the future but the loss of the past."

Kundera, who has lived in France since 1975, has given a great deal of thought to memory, and not out of idle curiosity. In one of his finest novels, *The Book of Laughter and Forgetting*, he managed to convey how the Soviet masters of Czechoslovakia and their Czech satraps went about depriving his countrymen of memory and making them children. They *organized* forgetting so that they could rewrite the past with few taking note. The names of political opponents and historical figures, the memory of whom posed a threat to Communist power, were simply thrown down the memory hole. And so were the inconvenient names of streets and institutions. Not only individuals, Kundera had reason to know, but nations too can lose their selves if they do not resist every attempt to make them forget their past and to believe lies. In very important ways, baseball encourages in us the habit of remembering, and thus it helps to prevent us from forgetting who we are.

Winning

THE HALL-OF-FAME UMPIRE JOCKO CONLAN WATCHED THOMSON'S homer from his station around first base. "I don't want to be a second-guesser," he said years later, "but in the Polo Grounds when the other team had the tieing [*sic*] runs on base you *had* to have a curve-ball pitcher. It was 4-2 and there were two men on, and Thomson's homer made it 5-4 Giants. I never thought he'd [Manager Dressen] bring in a fast-ball pitcher at a time like that."

I must have been nine or ten when my father, a wholesale florist in Chicago, took me to meet Jocko in the retail florist shop he had opened to supplement his income. I remember him as a short, kindly man who, when he learned that Andy Pafko was one of my favorite Cubs, promised to have him autograph a ball for me. Jocko thought Pafko "a fine guy—he never bothered anybody, and he was a solid ballplayer." It was not long before I was the envy of my friends. When I look at that ball, and Pafko's signature, memories come flooding back—of my father, of Wrigley Field, of baseball in the late 1940s and 1950s, of postwar America.

It was Buck O'Neil, the wonderful man about whom more in due course, who said, "Isn't it funny? Everybody remembers going to their first baseball game with their father. They might not remember going to their first day of school with their mother. They don't remember their first football game or their first Thanksgiving dinner. But they always remember going to the baseball game with their father." He was right.

On the shelf next to the ball Pafko signed for me is another, one that Jocko toted from ballpark to ballpark after promising my father that he would collect as many autographs

9

as the sphere's finite surface would accommodate. As good as his word, he soon presented me with a priceless gift: an official National League baseball signed by some of the greatest players of the era: Stan Musial, Pee Wee Reese, Johnny Mize, Warren Spahn, Harry "The Cat" Brecheen, Ewell "The Whip" Blackwell, Marty Marion, Johnny Sain.

This was the most memorable era in the game's history, "a time," in the words of Donald Kagan, Sterling Professor of Classics and History at Yale University, "of heroic greatness and consistent excellence." In a famous debate with George Will, pundit and celebrity baseball fan who prefers the contemporary game, Kagan dismissed the idea that success on the field resulted primarily from hard work and information gathering, that playing baseball was simply a "craft" much like any other. In fact, he rightly argued, it is primarily a result of natural ability. Think of Willie Mays or Mickey Mantle or Joe DiMaggio.

"No one," Kagan says, "ever thought that DiMaggio's greatness came chiefly from intelligence, care and hard work. Millions of people have those admirable qualities without significant result. Heroes arise by means of natural talents that are beyond the rest of us; the secret of their success is mysterious and charismatic." And so it was with Roy Hobbs, the tragic hero of Bernard Malamud's novel, *The Natural*. "He was," the press said of that mythic figure, "a throwback to a time of true heroes . . . a natural not seen in a dog's age, and weren't they the lucky ones he had appeared here and now to work his wonders before them?"

Early in Malamud's novel, a mentally ill woman invites Hobbs to her Chicago hotel room—and shoots him. That, as Malamud knew, was what had happened to Eddie Waitkus, a former Chicago Cub who in 1949 was playing first base for the Philadelphia Phillies. When in Chicago, the Phillies stayed at the Edgewater Beach Hotel. It was there that Waitkus received a note from a woman asking him to come to her room—she had something of great importance to tell him. He made the mistake of going. "If I can't have him," Ruth Ann Steinhagen later told the authorities, "nobody else can. And I decided I would kill him."

10

She almost did, but—miraculously—Waitkus survived, and the following year he helped the Phillies win the National League pennant. Playing in all 154 games, he hit .284 and drove home 44 runs, even though he had been moved to the lead-off spot in the batting order.

Waitkus was a fine player, but not a "natural." He joined the Cubs in 1941 but played in only 12 games before being shipped to Tulsa in the Texas League. In 1942, he played for the Los Angeles Angels and led the Pacific Coast League in hitting. Before he could rejoin the parent club for the 1943 season, Waitkus was drafted and served with distinction in the Pacific Theater; he earned numerous medals, including four Bronze Stars. The years away from the game did not seem to lessen his skills—he hit .304 in 1946, .292 in 1947, and .295 in 1948. After Pafko, he was the Cubs' best player. Nevertheless, in December 1948, the Cubs, displaying their usual genius for dealing, packed him and pitcher Hank Borowy off to Philadelphia in exchange for pitchers Dutch Leonard and Walt Dubiel. Waitkus was off to a .306 start when Steinhagen shot him.

We know who the real-life Roy Hobbs was: Shoeless Joe Jackson. Jackson was born in South Carolina in 1889 and never learned to read or write, but he was a natural on the diamond. By the time he joined the Philadelphia Athletics in 1908, he had picked up his nickname; in a minor league game, he took off his tight-fitting shoes and played in his stocking feet. After appearing in a few games in 1909, he reported to the New Orleans Pelicans of the Southern Association. At the end of the season the Athletics traded him to the Cleveland Naps (later the Indians). In 1911, his first full season in the big leagues, he batted .408. Swinging his favorite bat, Black Betsy, from the left side, Jackson finished his abbreviated career with a lifetime average of .356, third best in baseball history. Babe Ruth called him "the greatest natural hitter I ever saw" and imitated his swing.

In 1915, the Indians traded Jackson to the Chicago White Sox and, after a slow start, he began to swing Black Betsy with authority. He hit .341 in 1916 and .301 in 1917, a year in which the

White Sox won the American League pennant and went on to defeat the New York Giants in the World Series; Jackson hit a solid .304 in the fall classic. He hit .354 in 1918 and .351 the following year. That was one reason why the White Sox were listed as prohibitive favorites in the World Series against the Cincinnati Reds.

But as almost everyone knows, the White Sox lost the Series under more than suspicious circumstances. In due course, Jackson and seven of his teammates stood accused of a fix for what, in those days, amounted to a large sum of money. Jackson admitted to taking $5,000 from gamblers but claimed that he never gave less than his all on the field. He hit .375 and played errorless ball in the field, but his average in the five games that the White Sox lost was only .268. All of the accused, save "Chick" Gandil, who left the team to play semi-pro ball, played the 1920 season, but rumors of a fix continued to fly. With one series remaining in the season, White Sox owner Charles Comiskey suspended the seven suspects. Under pressure, Jackson confessed to having "helped throw games by muffing hard chances in the outfield or by throwing slowly to the infield." Pitcher Eddie Cicotte admitted that he "gave Cincinnati batters good balls to hit. I put them right over the plate. . . . I deliberately threw late to second on several plays." All eight players were indicted.

Because of a lack of conclusive evidence—Jackson and Cicotte recanted their confessions—the players were acquitted, but a shadow now hung over the game. The owners chose Judge Kenesaw Mountain Landis as baseball's first commissioner and the stern jurist delivered a different verdict. "Regardless of the verdict of juries, no player who throws a ball game, no player who undertakes or promises to throw a ball game, no player who sits in confidence with a bunch of crooked ballplayers and gamblers, where the ways and means of throwing a game are discussed and does not promptly tell his club about it, will ever play professional baseball." Landis banned all eight for life.

In *The Natural*, Roy Hobbs has a special bat—Wonderboy— and he reluctantly agrees to throw a pennant-deciding game for money needed to win a woman who held him in human bondage. During the game, he changes his mind, but it is too late—and few are deceived. The commissioner of baseball issues a statement: If reports of a fix are true, it "is the last of Roy Hobbs in organized baseball. He will be excluded from the game and all his records forever destroyed." A boy in the street turns to Roy: "Say it ain't true, Roy." The novel concludes with these tragic words: "When Roy looked into the boy's eyes he wanted to say it wasn't but couldn't, and he lifted his hands to his face and wept many bitter tears." When Shoeless Joe emerged from the Chicago courtroom in which he had been acquitted, a boy addressed plaintive words to him that will forever remain in baseball's—and America's—historical memory: "Say it ain't so, Joe."

Jackson, who always denied the story about the boy, never played another major league game, but he continues to stir the imagination of biographers and novelists. In 1982, W. P. Kinsella published *Shoeless Joe*, a novel about an Iowa farmer who constructs a partial baseball field on his land because of a voice that tells him that "if you build it, he [Jackson] will come." Jackson and the other seven Black Sox do appear, at least to the dreamlike eye of the farmer and others who share his willingness and ability to suspend disbelief. The novel is about many things, including dreams, imagination, hope, and reality of a special kind. But even more, it is about memory.

The farmer—who is, before anything else, a baseball fan who knows the history of the game—tries to explain to his traveling companion, "J. D. Salinger," why they must seek to learn about the life of "Moonlight" Graham, who in 1905 played one inning of major league ball. Memories of his brief career and later life will serve to stimulate their imagination and help them to experience realities of a higher order than those of the everyday. "We are mixing a cocktail of memories, and history, and love, and imagination," he says. "Now we must wait and see what effect it will have on us." It clearly had an effect on Kinsella himself, for he demonstrates a profound appreciation for the power of memory.

* * *

Although Mickey Mantle was only at the start of his amazing career when Malamud was writing *The Natural*, he was the greatest natural the game has ever known. As a high school boy, Mantle sustained a football injury that led to the development of osteomyelitis, a bone disease that handicapped him for the rest of his life. Nevertheless, the Yankees signed him to a contract on the day he graduated in 1949. The parent club called him up from Class C ball in the spring of 1951—and the rest is baseball history. Despite persistent and nagging problems with his legs—he sustained a serious knee injury in the 1951 World Series—Mantle performed feats that seemed not quite human. He could, for example, sprint from home to first in 3.1 seconds when swinging from the left side. He had huge forearms and could rifle the ball from anywhere in the outfield. I once saw him throw the ball on a line from deep center field in the old Comiskey Park (home of the Chicago White Sox) into the net far behind home plate. And it was only a pregame warm-up toss.

But it was at the plate that the switch-hitting Mantle was most awesome. He hit 536 career home runs, some of which were orbital. On April 17, 1953, he unloaded on a fastball (or was it a slider?) from Washington left-hander Chuck Stobbs. The ball clipped a beer sign on its way out of Griffith Stadium and came to rest in a backyard, 565 feet away—or so Red Patterson, the Yankees' public relations man, claimed. If so, it remains the longest home run ever actually measured (it inspired the expression "tape-measure home run"), although Mantle hit six that were even longer according to mathematical calculations. When it was recovered, the ball that Mantle hit off Stobbs was found to be deformed. On that day truth approached fiction; for in *The Natural*, Roy Hobbs once knocks the cover off the ball.

Nineteen-sixty-one was another banner year for Mantle; he batted .317 and drove in 128 runs. More important, he slugged 54 home runs and mounted a serious challenge to Ruth's record 60. It was a most extraordinary summer, because the man who hit in front of him, Roger Maris, was also chasing the Babe. I remember that the captain of the ship on which I was returning to the U.S.

from Europe posted daily reports of the M&M Boys' attempts to make history. In the end, Maris did. Born Roger Eugene Maras— the family was Croatian—Maris played 12 seasons in the majors. He compiled a respectable but hardly eye-popping batting average of .260, drove in 851 runs, and hit 275 homers. Sixty one of his round-trippers came in 1961.

For precisely that reason, sportswriters and "fans" put Maris through hell. As he drew steadily closer to the magical 60th, he earned the enmity not only of those who regarded the Babe's record as sacred but of those who had rather belatedly warmed to "The Mick." Such fans were not happy when an infected leg forced Mantle to drop out of the race. Under constant pressure and a hostility so relentless that it eventually made his hair fall out, the introverted Maris wished only to be left to do his job in peace. "Why can't they understand?" he pleaded in vain. "I don't want to be Babe Ruth. He was a great ballplayer. I'm not trying to replace him. The record is there, and damn right I want to break it, but that isn't replacing Babe Ruth."

As fate would have it, the American League had that very year lengthened its regular season from 154 to 162 games. Commissioner Ford Frick, who had been close to Ruth, let it be known that a distinction would be made between records established in 154 and those set in 162 games. Pressure was thus placed on Maris to break the record, if he could, in 154 games; on September 20, he hit number 59 off Baltimore's Milt Pappas in the Yankees' 154th game. That left him one shy of the record. Nevertheless, Maris refused to abandon the chase. On September 26, he hit number 60 off Baltimore's Jack Fisher—that shot came in game 159. In the final contest of the season, October 1, the Yankees faced the Boston Red Sox and Tracy Stallard. Could Maris break the record? Would it *be* a new record? Maris did not bother to think it over; early in the game, he took Stallard deep.

In 1961, Roger Maris hit 61 home runs and broke Babe Ruth's record. Yes, he had the advantage of a longer season. On the other hand, he was under far greater pressure. Since then, others— Mark McGwire, Sammy Sosa, and Barry Bonds—have advanced claims to a new record. Their claims should not be taken seriously. On January 11, 2010, McGwire, the new batting coach of the St. Louis Cardinals, admitted what everyone had assumed: he used steroids for many years, including his "record-breaking" season of 1998. "Looking back," he said in a carefully crafted statement, "I wish I had never played during the steroid era." As though he were not one of the principal architects of that era!

It is as certain as anything can be that Sosa and Bonds were also aided by chemicals. Like Hank Aaron, who broke the Babe's career home run record, Roger Maris played it honestly; he is still the true season record holder. It is nothing short of tragic that, as the late David Halberstam put it, he was "cast as an ordinary player who had the temerity to break a record of which he was not worthy." An example of how winning can, at the same time, be a form of losing.

* * *

Nineteen-fifty-one, the year that Maris's more famous teammate, Mickey Mantle, arrived in the big leagues, was the final year for Joe DiMaggio, not quite the natural that The Mick was but probably the last player to attain truly mythic status. "I must be worthy of the great DiMaggio who does all things perfectly," says the old man in Ernest Hemingway's *The Old Man and the Sea*. Fans knew of his multiple talents, legendary grace, and quiet dignity, without being told much about his personal life. "It was DiMaggio's good fortune," Halberstam once wrote, "to play in an era when his better qualities, both athletic and personal, were amplified, and his lesser qualities simply did not exist."

We remember the Yankee Clipper for many remarkable feats, but especially for setting a record that will never be broken—hitting safely in 56 straight games. Known simply as "The Streak," it was, according to the late paleontologist and Yankee fan Stephen Jay Gould, "the most extraordinary thing that ever happened in American sports." That is so because, as Michael Seidel put it in his book on the streak, which extended from May 15 to July 17, 1941, "the individual effort required for a personal hitting

16

streak is comparable to what heroic legend calls the *aristeia*, whereby great energies are gathered for a day, dispensed, and then regenerated for yet another day in an epic wonder of consistency." His intent, Seidel wrote, was "to inscribe DiMaggio's great streak in a context worthy of the memories it evokes."

Like Thomson's home run, DiMaggio's streak has about it a timeless quality. But it was also temporal, in the sense that it brings to mind dramatic historical events from the summer of 1941. On June 22, the Detroit Tigers were in New York to play the Yankees. In the sixth inning, DiMaggio powered an offering from Hal Newhouser over the right field fence, thereby extending his hitting streak to 35 games. This day, however, the news that the streak was still alive was trumped by reports that, early in the morning, Hitler had sent his armies into Soviet Russia, his ally during the first two years of the war in Europe. In the days and weeks ahead, reports of horrendous fighting reached an America still at uneasy peace. Baseball writer Robert W. Creamer remembers those reports, but his attention was focused on other matters. "Is this the heritage of the hapless baseball fan," he asked in his book on the game in 1941, "that he remembers 1941 for Joe DiMaggio and Ted Williams and Mickey Owen instead of Pearl Harbor?"

"Baseball," George Will has written, "is a game of episodic action. Discrete events standout." So they do. In 1941, Ted Williams produced two events that will always stand out. The first came in that year's All-Star Game, played in Detroit's Briggs Stadium; the date was July 8. Williams, who was to become one of the greatest—many would say *the* greatest—hitters in the history of the game, was batting .405 at the break, and manager Del Baker (Detroit Tigers) assigned him to the clean-up spot in the batting order, behind DiMaggio. The score stood 5-3 in favor of the National League as the American League came to bat in the last of the ninth. Claude Passeau of the Cubs was on the mound for the Nationals.

Passeau retired the first batter, but Ken Keltner, the Cleveland Indians' outstanding third baseman, hit a hard grounder to short that Eddie Miller could not handle. The Yankees' Joe Gordon then singled to right, and Passeau walked Cecil Travis to load the bases. DiMaggio strode to the plate and hit what looked like a double-play ball to Miller, but Miller's throw to second baseman Billy Herman was off line. Herman's hurried relay was wide, and the Yankee Clipper was safe at first. Keltner crossed home—the score was now 5-4. Passeau had then to face Williams. He ran the count to 2-1 before delivering a fastball that Williams sent into the upper right-field stands. "The Kid," as he was then known, clapped his hands and jumped up and down as he circled the bases; he had given his team a 7-5 victory. At the end of his illustrious career, he said that that blast was "the most thrilling hit of my life. It was a wonderful, wonderful day for me."

As the 1941 season neared an end, Williams's batting average hovered around the .400 mark. With only a Sunday double header in Philadelphia left on the schedule, he was hitting .39955, which baseball—but not the press—would have rounded off to .400. The question then arose: Should he sit out Sunday's games? Red Sox manager Joe Cronin offered to take his gifted hitter out of the lineup, but Williams would not hear of it. Cronin was worried and Williams was nervous as he walked to the plate for the first time in game one. It helped when the A's catcher Frankie Hayes spoke to him. "Mr. Mack [A's manager Connie Mack] says we're not to make it easy for you, Ted. But we're going to pitch to you." They did, and by the end of the long day Williams had collected six hits in eight trips to the plate, lifting his average to .406 (technically, .4057). No one has hit .400 or better since.

In the wake of the Japanese attack on Pearl Harbor, Williams initially sought, and was granted, a draft deferment on grounds that his mother depended upon him for support. After receiving bad press, he waited no longer than May 1942 to volunteer as a naval aviator. He did not have to report for duty until after the baseball season, one in which he batted .356, pounded out 36 homers, and drove in 137 runs. That was good enough to win the Triple Crown and to solidify his reputation as a slugger who could hit for average. In November, "The Kid" went on active duty, and for the next three years he served his country, primarily as a flight instructor. Before he could see combat the war ended, and he was relieved of duty in January 1946.

By the time the 1946 season opened, Williams was no longer a "kid." Like the Cleveland Indians' great hurler Bob Feller, who joined the Navy the day after Pearl Harbor, he was a man ready to pick up where he left off. Over the long summer he hit .342, homered 38 times, drove in 123 runs, and helped the Red Sox post a record of 104-50, good enough to win the American League pennant by 12 games. He and his teammates were favored to beat the National League champion St. Louis Cardinals in the World Series, and there were moments when it looked as though they would. In one of the most memorable of Series, the two teams split the first six games and were knotted at three going into the bottom—the St. Louis—half of the eighth inning of game seven.

Red Sox right hander Bob Klinger began by giving up a single to Cardinal outfielder Enos "Country" Slaughter, but he managed to retire the next two batters. The count on Harry "The Hat" Walker was 2-1 when the left-handed hitter poked a hit over shortstop Johnny Pesky's head into left-center field. What followed is one of the most discussed moments in World Series history. Slaughter was off and running with the pitch to Walker and never hesitated as he rounded the bases. Instead of firing the ball home, centerfielder Leon Culberson, in for the injured and more talented Dom DiMaggio, lobbed a relay to Pesky, whose back was to the infield.

Because of the roar of the crowd, the shortstop could not hear cries to hurry his throw. He *seemed* to hold the ball for a moment before firing it several feet up the line toward third. Slaughter slid home unmolested. His "Mad Dash" put the Cardinals ahead to stay, and Pesky, never a shirker, accepted full blame. "If I was alert," he told reporters after the game, "I'd have had him. When I finally woke up and saw him running for home, I couldn't have gotten him with a .22."

Pesky's teammates DiMaggio and Bobby Doerr always maintained that Culberson was the real goat, and he probably was. But no Series is ever won or lost because of one play. Had Williams had a good, or even a so-so, Series, the Red Sox might well have prevailed. But the Splendid Splinter hit a miserable .200, with no homers and one RBI. His poor performance offered fans, reporters, and teammates an opportunity to turn their critical sights on him. He seemed to many to be more concerned with his batting average than with his team's fortunes. Moreover, he never made a secret of his lack of interest in playing defense, and he refused to acknowledge fans' applause when he hit a home run. On the other hand, he often "acknowledged" their boos. In the early 1950s, I saw him in Comiskey Park. The White Sox's stylish lefty Billy Pierce struck him out three times. After the third failure, Williams responded to boos by tossing his bat straight up in the air, perhaps as high as two stories.

Some of the criticism leveled at Williams was justified . . . and yet, and yet. The man had his virtues. He gave freely of his time and raised money for The Jimmy Fund, which supports the fight against cancer in children—and he always refused to have his efforts publicized. He served in World War II and, on May 1, 1952, reported for duty during the Korean War—without complaint. As a Marine captain, he learned to fly the F-9 Panther and flew 39 combat missions in Korea, risking his life and sacrificing more of his career. And a storied career it was.

Williams's excellence was as remarkable as it was consistent. In 1957, the year he turned 39, he hit a superlative .388 and hammered 38 home runs. Two seasons later, it looked as though he had reached the end; he batted a mere .254 (the first and only time that his season average dropped below .300), with 10 round trippers. Not willing to end on such a dismal note, he returned for a final season and regained his form; he finished at .316, with 29 home runs and 72 runs batted in. The last game in which he appeared, played on September 28, 1960 in Boston's Fenway Park, was immortalized in a classic essay published by the late John Updike in the *New Yorker*.

Like every other fan at Fenway that fall day, Updike hoped to see Williams hit the ball out one last time. But until he stepped to the plate in the bottom of the eighth, there had been no miracle. Oriole pitcher Jack Fisher missed with his first pitch, and Williams waved at the second. Updike described what happened next:

> Fisher threw the third time, Williams swung again, and there it was. The ball climbed on a diagonal line into the vast volume of air over center field. From my angle, behind third base, the ball seemed less an object in flight than the tip of a towering, motionless construct, like the Eiffel Tower or the Tappan Zee Bridge. It was in the books while it was still in the sky.

Was Williams, as he aspired to be, the greatest hitter of all time? This is the kind of question for which those who love the game live. Ty Cobb hit for a higher average and Babe Ruth demonstrated more power. Still, as Updike argued, it was the *combination* of average and power that made Williams stand out. And if he had not missed more than four years because of military service, his numbers would be even greater. A lifetime average of .344 and a total of 521 home runs are, however, remarkable enough.

In Kinsella's *Shoeless Joe*, there is a moment when "Ray Kinsella," the novel's main character, has managed to summon "Moonlight" Graham, now a small-town doctor (which in fact he did become), to life. Graham had died in 1965, but "Kinsella" finds himself and the kindly physician—this according to town residents—in conversation. But what year had Kinsella entered imaginatively (or in reality)? He knows how to find out. "That was quite a World Series last fall!" he says to the aging Graham. "You can say that again," says the doctor. "I don't know when I've ever been prouder of the Giants" (the team for which he played an inning). "How about that Willie Mays? Did you see that catch? I went back to the movie theater three times to watch it on the newsreel." The year, then, is 1955.

Mays made what is now simply referred to as "The Catch" on September 29, 1954, in the Polo Grounds; it was game one of the

World Series against the Cleveland Indians. Working in the top of the eighth, Giant right hander Sal Maglie had put Indians on first and second. With the left-handed hitting Vic Wertz coming to the plate, Manager Leo Durocher called lefty Don Liddle out of the bullpen. Wertz worked the count to two balls and a strike before driving a shoulder-high fastball on a line to center field. Mays turned at the crack of the bat and ran with his back to the infield. At the last moment, according to sportswriter Arnold Hano who attended the game, he "put his hands up in cup-like fashion over his left shoulder, and caught the ball much like a football player catching leading passes in the end zone."

Jocko Conlan happened to be umpiring at second base that day. It was a splendid catch, Jocko later recalled, but the Giants' center fielder had made others as good or better. What he did *after* making the catch was what was truly amazing. As Mays pulled the ball in, "he spun around and threw the ball, all in one motion. His hat fell off, and he fell to the ground, but the ball came in to the infield on a line all the way from the center-field fence. It kept a run from scoring that would have given Cleveland the ballgame. I watched that ball come in and I said to myself, 'This has got to be the best throw anybody could ever make.' The catch and the throw together was the play of the series, but the throw was even better than the catch." Thanks to Mays, Liddle could, with a smile, say to Marv Grissom, who relieved him, "Well, I got *my* man!"

The Indian runner on second base that day was center fielder Larry Doby, a man at the center of another historic event—the breaking of the color line in the American League. It is a pity that relatively few Americans remember him, overshadowed as he is by Jackie Robinson. As everyone knows, Robinson was the first black player to enter the modern major leagues, and he quickly distinguished himself as a hitter, fielder, and fierce competitor. Only eleven weeks after Robinson made his debut, Indians' owner Bill Veeck signed Doby to a contract. The Negro League standout played in his first major league game on July 5, 1947. Nervous and overeager, he appeared in only 28 more games during the season and hit an anemic .156.

Far more reserved than Robinson, Doby was nevertheless sensitive to racial slights. In fact, such slights were rare on the field; most—not all—of his teammates and the members of other teams welcomed him and treated him with respect. It was, he later recalled, "the conditions I had to live with away from the ball park. They burned me up inside. If you're an introvert, which I probably am, your feelings stay inside." Throughout most of his career, Doby had to stay in hotels or homes away from his teammates. "Not many people realize this," he recalled, "but I was segregated in spring training for 10 out of 13 years, right through the spring of 1959." That hurt.

Nevertheless, Doby carved out an outstanding career. Originally an infielder, Indian manager Lou Boudreau switched him to center field, and he became one of the best in the business. In 1948, he hit .301, with 14 home runs and 66 runs batted in. He helped lead the Indians to the pennant and a World Series victory over the Boston Braves. In 1950 he had his best year at the plate, hitting .326, with 25 home runs and 102 runs batted in. In 1954, his average dropped to .272, but he slugged 32 home runs and drove in 126. He contributed greatly to the record 111 wins that put the Indians in the World Series against the Giants—and that the National Leaguers swept.

By the time Doby's playing career ended on July 26, 1959, he had posted a lifetime batting average of .283, hit 253 home runs—some of them true tape-measure shots—and driven in 970 runs. He went on to a career as a batting instructor. And for a short time he managed the Chicago White Sox—the second black man (after Frank Robinson) to guide a team. Nevertheless, he had every reason to feel underappreciated, not only as a pioneer but as a splendid performer. Justice was finally done when in 1998 the Veterans Committee elected him to the Hall of Fame.

When the Indians won the World Series in 1948, Cleveland honored team members with a parade through the city's streets. Riding next to Doby in an open convertible was outfielder Dale Mitchell, a fine player who was later to be a principal in one of baseball's most unforgettable moments. A left-handed hitter, Mitchell broke in with the Indians in September 1946; he hit .432 in 11 games. In 1947, his first full season, he hit .316, and in 1948 he led the team with an average of .336, third best in the league behind Ted Williams and Lou Boudreau. A contact hitter, Mitchell rarely struck out, a fact of importance for what was to come. Near the end of the 1956 season, the Indians sold his contract to the Brooklyn Dodgers, who went on to win the pennant and to face the New York Yankees in the World Series.

It was in game five of the Series that Mitchell secured a place in history—to his everlasting regret. The Dodgers were the defending World Champions, thanks to a brilliant pitching performance by Johnny Podres and a memorable catch by left-fielder Sandy Amoros in game seven of the 1955 Series. The 1956 Series stood at two games apiece when Don Larsen, an inconsistent hurler with chronic control problems, went to the mound for the Yankees. His opponent on that Monday, October 8, was Sal Maglie, no longer in his prime, but still a big-game pitcher.

Larsen had finished the regular season with four straight victories and an 11-5 overall record; his earned run average was a respectable 3.25. This inspired confidence in manager Casey Stengel, but Larsen had lasted only 1 2/3 innings in game two, a consequence of issuing passes to four of the first nine batters he faced. On that day, the no-wind-up delivery he had begun to use did nothing to improve his control. In game five, however, it blessed him with a miraculous ability to put the ball exactly where catcher Yogi Berra wanted it. Of the 97 pitches he threw that afternoon, 70 were strikes. When it was all over, Larsen had pitched the only perfect game in World Series history—27 batters up, 27 down. No Dodger reached first base.

There had been other perfect games before, and there have been more since, but never in a World Series. And this was an outstanding Dodger team. The lineup that Larsen handcuffed: Jim "Junior" Gilliam, a fine switch-hitter (the Dodgers later retired his number 19), at second base; Pee Wee Reese at shortstop; Duke Snider in center field; Jackie Robinson at third base; Gil Hodges at first base; Sandy Amoros in left field; Carl Furillo in right field; Roy Campanella behind the plate; Maglie on the mound. Throwing only fastballs and sliders, Larsen had the Dodgers talking to themselves.

To be sure, he did dodge a couple of bullets. In the second inning, Robinson smashed a ball between third and short. Yankee third baseman Andy Carey leaped high but managed only to tip the ball with his glove. As shortstop Gil McDougald moved into the hole, the ball dropped in front of him. Quickly he picked it up and fired to first baseman Joe Collins just in time to nip number 42. "We would have never gotten Robinson out," Carey said later, "if the game would have been played two or three years earlier when he still had his speed."

In the fifth, Hodges lined a shot to left center, but Mickey Mantle made a running back-handed catch that he himself called his greatest. An inning earlier, The Mick had driven a Maglie curve ball into the right-field seats. The Yankees added an insurance run in the sixth, but Larsen did not need it.

As the game progressed, the pressure mounted. No Yankee would speak to Larsen, much less mention the fact that he was pitching a no-hitter—in those days, it was still regarded as a jinx to do so. As Larsen walked to the mound for the ninth inning, fans in Yankee Stadium and throughout the United States held their breath. Like many other high school students, I managed to listen on a transistor radio. Carl Furillo, the Dodger right fielder with the rifle arm, flied out to Hank Bauer in right. One away. Roy Campanella then hit Larsen's second pitch on the ground to Billy Martin at second. Two men out. Maglie was due up next, but manager Walter Alston sent Dale Mitchell to the plate in his stead. Vin Scully told the television audience what it already knew: "I think it would be safe to say no man in the history of baseball has ever come up to home plate in a more dramatic moment."

Mitchell took Larsen's first offering for a ball. Umpire Babe Pinelli, in the final game of his career, called the next pitch a strike. He later told Duke Snider that "he wanted to go out on a no-hitter in a World Series. . . . So anything close was a strike." Mitchell swung and missed the third pitch—the count stood at 1 and 2. Determined to swing at anything close to the plate, Mitchell fouled off the next pitch. With everyone's nerves stretched to the limit, Larson uncorked a fastball. Mitchell started to swing, tried to hold up, and heard Pinelli yell "strike three." To this day, controversy swirls around that final pitch—was it in the strike zone or was it high and outside, as Yankee players on the field later testified?

Difficult to tell from the film footage, but it was clearly close enough. "I guess," Mitchell said later, "I should have swung." In fact, Berra was probably right when he insisted that the Dodger pinch hitter had in any case committed himself. Poor Dale! "Here," he lamented, "I average better than .300 for a career, get more than 200 hits in a season twice, play on three pennant winners, and all people remember me for now is that I took a called third strike to give Don Larsen his perfect game in the World Series." He never got over it, and in his last years—he died at 65 in 1987—he drank heavily.

Don Larsen continued his major league career until 1967, when he stayed for a cup of coffee (three games) with the Cubs. He retired in 1968 after a brief time in the minors. His final major league record: 81 wins and 91 losses. In five World Series, he won four and lost two. Not exactly a Hall of Fame career. And yet, for one fall day in 1956, he was perfect. "Ladies and gentlemen," Vin Scully said, "it's the greatest game ever pitched in baseball history."

Perhaps so, but Scully could not then know that on May 26, 1959, the Pittsburgh Pirates' Harvey Haddix would pitch twelve perfect innings in Milwaukee's County Stadium against the defending National League champion Braves—only to lose the game in the 13th! Haddix was 12-12 that year and posted a career won-lost record of 136-113 with five clubs—nothing about which to be embarrassed, but not nearly good enough to put him in Cooperstown. And yet on that cool evening in May he allowed no one to reach first base for three innings beyond regulation play—and that against a lineup that boasted Eddie Mathews, Hank Aaron, Wes Covington, Andy Pafko (who seems to have had a knack for playing in historic contests), and Joe Adcock, whose double (actually the ball left the park but the Braves were guilty of a base-running miscue) in the 13th inning was the only hit that Haddix gave up. No one has ever matched the length of that perfection. But in 1991, Major League Baseball changed the definition of a no-hitter to "a game in which a pitcher or pitchers complete a game of nine innings or more without allowing a hit." The League therefore removed Haddix's performance from the list of perfect games.

Something similar befell Red Sox pitcher Ernie Shore in a game against the Washington Senators on June 23, 1917. Babe Ruth started the game for Boston and walked the first batter on four pitches. Enraged by the calls, the Babe took a swing at home umpire Brick Owens and was promptly ejected from the game; on came Shore. On his first pitch, the runner on first, Ray Morgan, was caught trying to steal second. Shore then proceeded to retire the next 26 batters in a row. A perfect game? A no-hitter? Neither, according to Major League Baseball.

Shore had a 65-43 career record. Not too bad, but not a ticket to the Hall of Fame. Perfect games are rarities, and it seems, for some odd reason, that they are disproportionately the property of so-so hurlers. And speaking of mediocre hurlers who performed miraculous feats, what about Johnny Vander Meer, the Cincinnati left-hander who hurled back-to-back no-hitters (neither of which was perfect) in 1938? Vander Meer was in his first full season in the majors when he went to the mound in Cincinnati's Crosley Field on June 11. Although he had trouble with his control—he walked three men—he no-hit the Boston Bees, managed by Casey Stengel.

Four days later, in the first night game ever played in Brooklyn's Ebbets Field (and with Babe Ruth and Jesse Owens in attendance), Vander Meer walked eight squinting Dodgers without surrendering a hit or a run. It is unlikely that his achievement will ever be matched—it is inconceivable that it will ever be surpassed (that is, three consecutive no-hitters). But Vander Meer's 13-year-career record was 119-121.

Not every no-hit pitcher was a journeyman. Take Hall of Famer Sandy Koufax for example. Koufax broke in with the Brooklyn Dodgers in June 1955, and as he began the 1961 season (the Dodgers had by then moved to Los Angeles) he had posted an unimpressive record of 36-40. He improved to 18-13 in 1961, and then something dramatic happened—he gained an almost complete mastery over his pitches. Over the next five years, before an arthritic elbow forced him to retire at the age of 30, he won 111 games, lost 34, and posted an ERA of 1.95. He was virtually untouchable. He had three no-hitters to his credit when, on the evening of September 9, 1965, he threw a perfect game against the Chicago Cubs.

In the Cubs' lineup that day were two future Hall of Fame players, Billy Williams and Ernie Banks, and one who *should be* in the Hall—Ron Santo. Koufax was not facing a weak-hitting club. To add to the challenge, Cub pitcher Bob Hendley gave up only one bloop hit and one unearned run. Nevertheless, Koufax had retired all 26 men to face him when veteran Harvey Kuenn walked to the plate. Kuenn was nearing the end of a fine career and had made the final out in Koufax's 1963 gem against the San Francisco Giants—but he rarely struck out. He worked the count to 2 and 2 before Vin Scully called the deciding pitch. "Sandy into his windup. Here's the pitch! Swung on and missed! A perfect game!"

Was Koufax the greatest pitcher in the game's history? Casey Stengel and many others thought so, but Branch Rickey did not. The "Mahatma" lived long enough to watch Koufax *and* Christy Mathewson pitch, and he told Roger Kahn that it would have been "sheer pleasure" to have either man on his staff. But, "taking nothing away from the younger fellow, I regard Mathewson as the finest pitcher who ever lived." Perhaps so, but for five years Koufax was more than a pitcher—he was an artist, a Cézanne of the mound. Relying on a fastball and a curve that was difficult to believe even when seen, he established complete dominance over his opposition. If he was not the greatest pitcher of all time, he was without doubt the greatest of *his* time. No one who was fortunate enough to see him pitch will ever forget the experience.

His achievements on the mound brought Koufax much unwanted attention. He was particularly irritated when, in his view, too much was made of his being Jewish. When *Time* magazine published an article saying the great left-hander liked to listen to Felix Mendelssohn's music—that wonderful composer having been of Jewish origin—Koufax seethed. "I listen to Sinatra a helluva lot more than I listen to Mendelssohn," he snarled. But if Koufax tried to discourage any talk of his ethnic background, the Cardinals' Bob Gibson, his most serious rival for the title of "greatest of his time," was perfectly willing to talk about being black in America.

Among his many achievements on the mound, Gibson no-hit the Pirates the night of August 14, 1971. Although he was no more than 6'1", he loomed larger on the mound; among the most athletic hurlers in baseball history, he seemed to throw his whole body toward home plate. "Intimidating" is the word that came most often to the lips of those whose misfortune it was to step into the batter's box against the intense right hander. He gave opponents—or "enemies"—what many of them referred to as "The Look," and he never spoke to them (and rarely to his teammates). He possessed an outstanding fastball and a devastating slider and never hesitated to brush back a hitter. Nor did he scruple to hit a batter who, in his view, trespassed upon parts of the plate that belonged to him. What made him even more fearsome was his practice of working so quickly on the mound that batters had little time to get set at the plate.

Gibson broke into the majors in 1959 and began to hit his stride in 1964, a year in which he won 19 and lost 12. With his help, the Cardinals won the pennant and prepared to face the Yankees in the World Series. He got the call in game two but lost to Mel Stottlemyre. With the Series tied 2-2, he again went to the mound and emerged victorious, striking out thirteen and walking two. In the seventh and deciding game, Gibson returned to the mound on two days' rest; although he began to tire in the late innings, he managed to hold on for a 7-5 victory. As a reward, he was voted the Series' Most Valuable Player.

Gibson went 20-12 in 1965 and 21-12 in 1966. In the following year, he suffered a broken leg as a result of a line drive off the bat of the great Roberto Clemente (when next he faced the Pirate outfielder, he decked him), but he still managed to win 13 games. In the World Series against the Red Sox, Gibson pitched three complete-game victories and was again the Series' MVP. In 1968, a year that changed American history, Gibson was untouchable. He won 22, lost 9, and posted an ERA of 1.12, a modern-day record. "Many observers (including this one)," Roger Angell has written, "believe that Gibson's 1.12 earned-run average in 1968 is one of the Everests of the game, ranking with Joe DiMaggio's fifty-six-consecutive-game hitting streak in 1941 and Hack Wilson's hundred and ninety runs batted in in 1930."

In game one of the 1968 World Series against Detroit's Tigers, Gibson struck out 17 batters, eclipsing Koufax's record of 15 strikeouts in game one of the 1963 Series. He went on to win game four, but lost game seven. When he retired in 1975, he could look back upon a career in which he notched 251 wins and lost 174; his ERA was a phenomenal 2.91. A proud man who resented racial prejudice, Gibson made his protest on the mound. After all the recognition he earned—including election to the Hall of Fame—it is a pity that he seems not to have found the peace he deserves. He was a pitcher for the ages.

"There is no one greatest pitcher," Roger Kahn has written, and that is no doubt true. It is certainly true that it is difficult to compare players from very different eras, though Kahn himself asked Branch Rickey to do just that. He did so because fans cannot help themselves. Such a discussion, or debate, is one of the pleasures the game affords. Of pitchers of an earlier era, Cy Young and Walter Johnson are always mentioned when the discussion turns to greatness, but I think it fair to say that Christy Mathewson would garner the most votes as the game's preeminent hurler—and as a model of what a ballplayer, indeed a man, ought to be. When it came both to pitching and to character, "Matty" was a winner.

Mathewson broke in with the New York Giants in 1900 and played for 17 years. It was a time when players were generally a coarse and unruly lot, many of them drunks, some illiterate. Matty, while not as saintly as many believed, was cut from different cloth. From a Christian family, the good-looking young man from Factoryville, Pennsylvania, attended Bucknell University for three years and compiled an outstanding record as a student. Throughout his life, he exhibited the kind of character that was in short supply during baseball's Dead Ball Era (roughly 1900–1919). All the more mysterious, then, was the close and lasting friendship he forged with John McGraw, who took over as manager of the Giants in 1902 and continued to direct the team for 33 years. A combative, profane, and hard-drinking Irishman, McGraw also had a taste, if not a knack, for gambling—an enthusiasm that was something of an occupational hazard for baseball men before the days of multimillion-dollar contracts.

Nevertheless, Matty was proud to call his manager his friend. The "Little Napoleon," as McGraw was called, may well have thought of his young right-hander as a son. He certainly thought of him as a meal ticket. Matty won 30 games in 1903, 33 the following year, and 31 in 1905. In the 1905 World Series against Connie Mack's Philadelphia Athletics, he performed a matchless feat of pitching, shutting the A's out three times in six days. It was no fluke. In the course of his remarkable career, he won 373 games (79 by shutouts) and lost only 188. He had a fourth 30-win season (37) in 1908. His lifetime ERA was 2.13. He made 551 starts and completed 434 of them. In 4,780.2 innings pitched, he issued an almost unbelievably low number of 844 bases on balls.

Obviously, precision control was one of the marks of Matty's pitching. He possessed an unparalleled ability to put the ball precisely where he wanted it. He threw a blazing fastball and what today would be called a slider, but he was most famous for the "fadeaway" (screwball) that curved away from left-handed batters. No one who threw as many innings as he did, or pitched so frequently with two days rest, could do so without pacing himself—and that is exactly what Mathewson did. He saved his best stuff for what he called "pinches," critical moments in a game. It is true that he had the advantage of pitching in the Dead Ball Era and therefore did not have to worry much about serving up gopher balls. On the other hand, he played at a time when the fields were not in the immaculate shape they are today. Furthermore, the players behind him wore very small gloves and could not make the kinds of catches that modern-day players can.

Mathewson was a member of a New York Giant team that won five National League Pennants and one World Championship, but neither he nor his latter-day rivals, Koufax and Gibson, played for the winningest team in major league history—the New York Yankees, owners of 40 American League Pennants and 27 World Championships. Originally the Baltimore Orioles (first season, 1901) the club became the New York Highlanders when it moved to Manhattan's Hilltop Park in 1903. Ten years later the Highlanders became the Yankees and moved to the Polo Grounds. In 1915, brewery heir Jacob Ruppert and his partner, Tillinghast L'Hommedieu Huston, bought the franchise from William Devery and the disreputable Frank Farrell; Ruppert bought Huston out in 1923.

The Yankees achieved little success before they began to acquire talent from Boston Red Sox owner Harry Frazee, who was strapped for cash. Frazee sold them pitchers Waite Hoyt and Herb Pennock and, in 1920, pitcher-turned-outfielder George Herman "Babe" Ruth. "I believe the sale of Babe Ruth will ultimately strengthen the team," he said. Those were the words of an unwise man. After sending the Babe to New York, the Red Sox experienced anything but good fortune; they would have to wait until 2004 before they won another World Series. The long dry spell was a result, according to popular belief, of the "Curse of the Bambino"—the wages of selling the Babe to the Yankees.

Ruth and the rest of the Yankee team assembled by General Manager Ed Barrow—a former Red Sox field general—and Manager Miller Huggins were certainly blessed; between 1921 and 1928 they won six pennants and three World Series. In 1923, they moved to "The House That Ruth Built" (so named by sportswriter Fred Lieb): Yankee Stadium in the Bronx.

In the opinion of many knowledgeable observers, the 1927 Yankee team was the greatest in history. In addition to Ruth and Lou Gehrig, the lineup (the "Murderers' Row") included center fielder Earle Combs, shortstop Mark Koenig, left fielder Bob Meusel, and second baseman Tony Lazzeri; Hoyt, Pennock, and Wilcy Moore anchored the pitching staff. Throughout the long summer, Ruth and Gehrig battled each other for the American League home run title. When it was over, Gehrig had 47 and the Babe a record 60. After besting his previous high of 59, Ruth shouted: "Let's see some son of a bitch try to top that one!" Thirty-four years later, Roger Maris, no SOB, did just that.

The home run derby proved to be more interesting than the pennant race. The Yankees finished with a record of 110 wins and 44 losses. The second place A's could do no better than 91-63. The Red Sox, under the "curse," finished last (51-103), 59 games off the Yankees' pace. The World Series that pitted the Yankees against the Pittsburgh Pirates was even more of a mismatch—the American Leaguers swept the shell-shocked National League winners.

Few baseball fans among the living were around to see the 1927 Yankees in action, but memory is collective—it can be, and often is, passed down from generation to generation. Hence it is *as if* we of a later time remember the Babe and Lou and the rest of that unforgettable team. The testimony of our fathers and grandfathers provide needed context for grainy films of the Babe and static-filled broadcasts of Lou giving his moving speech at the "Appreciation Day" in his honor on July 4, 1939. Terminally ill with amyotrophic lateral sclerosis ("Lou Gehrig's Disease"), the future Hall of Fame first baseman said, "Fans, for the past two weeks you have been reading about the bad break I got. Yet today I consider myself the luckiest man on the face of this earth. . . . I may have had a tough break, but I have an awful lot to live for."

The Ruth-Gehrig era did not end in 1927. The Yankees repeated as World Champions in 1928 and, after watching Connie Mack's Philadelphia A's capture three pennants in a row, reclaimed the league championship in 1932. Managed by Joe Mc-Carthy, the Yankees faced the Chicago Cubs in the World Series; it ended in a sweep for the Bronx Bombers. An otherwise unexciting Series is remembered for what happened, or did not happen, in game three, played in Wrigley Field.

It all began in 1930, when the Yankees traded Mark Koenig, shortstop on their 1927 World Championship team, to the Detroit Tigers, who dispatched him to the minor leagues in 1932. There he might have ended his career had the Cubs not had need of him. Their regular shortstop, Billy Jurges, had stopped two bullets from a gun belonging to an ex-girlfriend, and he faced an extended period of recovery. In 33 games with the North Siders, Koenig batted .353 and, as my father once verified for me, contributed materially to their success. His new teammates, however, viewed things differently; they voted him no more than a half World Series share.

Koenig's former teammates, the Yankees, were incensed and determined to make the Chicagoans pay. Ruth may have had the unappreciated shortstop in mind when he came to bat against Charlie Root in the fifth inning. Or he may have been upset by the verbal abuse heaped on him by the Cub bench. At any rate, after the count reached 2-2, he pointed to something: The center field bleachers? Root? The Cubs' bench? No one knows for certain. What we do know is that he blasted the next pitch some 440 feet into the bleachers in right center, and reporter Joe Williams claimed that Ruth had "called his shot" (though in later years he admitted to harboring doubts).

Not many in the stands agreed with him, and existing films of the turn at bat are inconclusive. Mark Koenig thought he was pointing toward the place where he had hit a previous homer. Pat Pieper, the Cubs' beloved public address announcer, testified that "Babe definitely pointed." As for Ruth himself, he was not the kind of man to kill a good story, especially about his prowess.

The Yankees did not win another pennant and World Series until 1936, the first year of the DiMaggio era (1936–51). During those years, the Yankee Clipper led his team to 11 pennants and 10 World Series Championships—losing only one Fall Classic, to the St. Louis Cardinals in 1942. Manager Joe McCarthy (1932–early 1946) could draw upon the talents of his peerless center fielder, Lou Gehrig (until he could no longer play), shortstop Frankie Crosetti, catcher Bill Dickey, and pitchers Red Ruffing and Lefty Gomez. He was in the dugout in 1941 when DiMaggio hit in 56 straight games, and his teams continued the Yankee tradition of winning.

By the time DiMaggio retired in 1951, Casey Stengel had taken over as manager and Mickey Mantle had appeared on the scene. In charge from 1949 to 1960, Stengel guided the Yankees to ten pennants and seven World Series victories. He was blessed with Mantle, catcher Yogi Berra, catcher Elston Howard, outfielder Hank Bauer, and pitchers Vic Raschi, Allie Reynolds, Eddie Lopat, and Whitey Ford. But despite his joking and his peculiar way of speaking ("Stengelese"), he had a genius for getting the most out of average players and those such as Johnny Mize and Enos Slaughter who were in the autumn of their careers.

"The Old Professor's" team lost the 1960 World Series to the Pittsburgh Pirates when Bill Mazeroski hit a game- and Series-winning "walk off" home run off Ralph Terry in the ninth inning of game seven, an iconic moment in baseball history. Believing Stengel to be too old to manage—he was 70—the Yankees forced his retirement. His departure was not the end of Yankee heroics. They were World Series winners in the early 1960s, late 1970s, and, under Joe Torre, the late 1990s, but after 2000 they went eight years without a title. Joe Girardi, who replaced Torre for the 2008 season, guided the team, led by Derek Jeter and Alex Rodriguez, to the 2009 championship, but somehow team members—who had worn and would wear several uniforms—did not seem to be in the same league with earlier Yankee champions.

Winners are not always loved, and countless baseball fans hate the Yankees—with a passion. Among them was Douglass Wallop, sometime journalist, novelist, and—poor man—Washington Senators fan. Born in the District in 1920, Wallop graduated from the University of Maryland. For five months in 1948, he took dictation from Dwight D. Eisenhower as the general set forth his account of the recently concluded *Crusade in Europe*. But it was fiction that Wallop wished to write and to which he devoted much of his life. He was able to do so largely because of the enormous success of his second novel, *The Year the Yankees Lost the Pennant* (1954).

While the 1940s–1950s Senators—sometimes called the Nationals—were mired in the second division, Wallop watched the Yankees win pennants in 1947, 1949, 1950, 1951, 1952, and 1953. Unable to alter reality, he imagined that in 1958 his beloved team would finally grasp the American League championship from the hated New Yorkers. They did so—in the novel—because they had in right field Joe Hardy, a player possessed of demonic talents. Literally. Young Joe was actually a 50-year-old real estate salesman and devoted Senators fan named Joe Boyd. On July 21, 1958, after the Senators suffer another loss, a Mr. Applegate appears and offers the middle-aged man a chance to become a baseball legend—and to lead the Senators to the pennant.

It is clear from the first moment that Applegate is Mephistopheles and that he is attempting to strike a Faustian bargain— youth and immense baseball talents in exchange for Joe's immortal soul. Wallop's reworking of the Faust legend lends to the novel a greater seriousness than he may have originally intended. The theme of selling one's soul for some godlike gift or power has attracted the attention of some of the greatest artists in Western culture: Christopher Marlowe, Johann Wolfgang von

Goethe, Thomas Mann, Hector Berlioz, Charles Gounod, Franz Liszt, and others.

In Wallop's version of the legend, Applegate agrees to append an escape clause to the "contract," secure in the belief that youth, fame, Senator victories, and the attentions of the beautiful Lola, who is also under contract, will make Hardy forget all about his wife Bess and his former life. But he fiendishly hides a relevant fact from Boyd/Hardy: He is a Yankee fan! What else would Mephistopheles be? At the last moment, he will see to it that the Yankees win another pennant, and in that way have his cake and eat it; the Senators and their fans will have their hopes dashed with triumph within their grasp. And in the most monstrous evil of all, he will see to it that Joe is traded to—the Yankees!

Innocent of these diabolical plans, Hardy leads the Washington team out of the second division and into a race for first place. Even before reaching the September 21 deadline for deciding whether or not he wishes to return to his former life, he clobbers 48 home runs and maintains an astronomical batting average of .545. In the third game of a series against the infamous Yankees, Joe unloads a tape-measure home run, "a feat accomplished previously only by the Messrs. Ruth, Gehrig, and Larry Doby, although surpassed in a somewhat different direction back in 1953 by the veteran Mickey Mantle, then of the Yankees and currently of the Cleveland Indians." Wallop could not abide the thought of The Mick playing for New York.

In the end, happy to report, the evil one is foiled. The Senators win the 1958 pennant and, thanks to Joe's stubborn goodness and Lola's true love, our hero is free to return to his wife even though the September 21 deadline has passed. A bit of melodrama but still moving, not least because it reflects a different time in America, a time when few would smirk at Wallop's description of Joe: "A man who had always lived a decent life [and] who had never cheated a client." It boiled down "to a matter of code, and Joe's code gave high importance to the matters of taking one's medicine, of lying in the bed one had made. It was sniveling to do otherwise."

The novel inspired the musical *Damn Yankees*, with music and lyrics by Richard Adler and Jerry Ross. The film version starred Ray Walston as Applegate and the marvelous Gwen Verdon as Lola. Choreography was by Bob Fosse, whom Verdon later married. Tab Hunter gave a surprisingly good performance as Joe Hardy. To its slight disadvantage, the musical deviates a bit from the novel, but the tunes ("You Gotta Have Heart," "Whatever Lola Wants") and dancing numbers are a joy.

Wouldn't you know it, the real-life Yankees won the pennant in 1958. The Senators? They finished last, with a record of 61-93.

Losing

> You can learn little from victory. You can learn everything from defeat.
>
> *Christy Mathewson*

WE BEGAN THESE REFLECTIONS BY RECALLING BOBBY THOMSON'S famous home run; "the Giants win the pennant," broadcaster Russ Hodges shouted repeatedly. Yes they did, but of course the Dodgers lost it. Don DeLillo put these insightful words into the mouth of one of his characters: "It's not about Thomson hitting the homer. It's about Branca making the pitch. It's all about losing." "Why me?" Branca cried. He did not smoke, did not cheat, and drank very little. He did not deserve his fate—and yet it *was* his fate. In *Why Me? A Philosophical Inquiry into Fate*, Michael Gelven points out that we are free agents, but we are also beings who receive "bestowals," such as the time and place of our birth, the identity of our parents, the color of our eyes. These are fates that have much to do with who we are but nothing to do with what we deserve.

A world in which everyone received only what he or she deserved would be a world of perfect justice. But that would mean not only that we would not experience any undeserved pain or suffering but that we would never receive any unearned good— wonderful parents, intelligence, good looks. Being vulnerable to fate is, in short, part of what it means to be a person. Ralph Branca was of course both an agent—he threw the pitch—and a recipient of a bestowal, a fate: he, not Labine or Erskine, was summoned from the bullpen. It must have been some small consolation to learn, as he did three years later, that the Giants had devised an almost comically elaborate method of stealing the catcher's signs, and that, in all probability, Thomson knew what pitch to expect. But one doubts that Branca would have been consoled by what Nicholas Dawidoff wrote in 2001: "Baseball is no different from Shakespeare and Chekhov, in that the most appealing stories are always tragic."

There is an element of truth in this, but not every baseball tragedy appeals. Consider another story mentioned by DeLillo—the suicide of Donnie Moore. Moore broke in with the Cubs in 1975 and later played for the Cardinals, Brewers, and Braves. In 1985, he signed as a free agent with the California Angels. A journeyman who had achieved minimal success, he saved 31 games for the West Coast team and was rewarded with a three-year, $3 million contract. He saved 21 games during the 1986 season and helped the Angels win the American League's West Division. They then faced the Boston Red Sox in the American League Championship Series.

The Angels led the series three games to one as they took the field for game five, played in Anaheim on October 12. They held a 5-2 advantage going into the ninth inning, needing only three more outs to win their first pennant. Boston's Bill Buckner led off the inning with a single to center, but Jim Rice struck out. That brought Don Baylor to the plate. He hit a 3-2 pitch from Angels' hurler Mike Witt for a home run; the score was now 5-4. The next hitter, Dwight Evans, popped out. Angel players and fans readied themselves for a celebration, but manager Gene Mauch, who had led teams to winning seasons but never to a championship, decided to remove Witt. He summoned left-hander Gary Lucas to pitch to left-handed hitter Rich Gedman. Lucas's first pitch struck Gedman on the forearm.

Coming to the plate was reserve center fielder Dave Henderson, who hit from the right side. Mauch decided to call for the right-handed Moore, whose first pitch to Henderson was low. He then threw two strikes, the second one swinging. Moore was one pitch away from sending his team to the World Series. He fired a fastball low. Henderson then fouled off two pitches. Moore then put everything he had into a split-finger fastball. Henderson swung. Al Michaels made the call for ABC: "Deep to left and [left-fielder Brian] Downing goes back. And it's gone! Unbelievable! You're looking at one for the ages here. Astonishing! Anaheim Stadium was one strike away from turning into Fantasyland! And now the Red Sox lead 6-5."

That was not the end of the game. The Angels tied the score in the bottom of the ninth and the game went into extra innings. With Moore still on the mound, the Red Sox loaded the bases in the eleventh—and Henderson again came to the plate. He hit Moore's first pitch on the fly to center, deep enough to score the runner from third. The Angels failed to score in their half of the inning and the Red Sox had a 7-6 victory. The California team still had a 3-2 lead in the series, but the next two games were to be played in Boston's Fenway Park; the Red Sox won both of them. So the Angels had their chances, but Henderson's home run, when they were one strike away from the World Series, seemed to make them lose heart.

It certainly made Moore lose heart—that and persistent back problems that limited his effectiveness in 1987, a year in which he saved only five games. At the end of the season he underwent surgery, but although it was successful he struggled in 1988. Many in the stands refused to forget "the pitch," and he had difficulty getting anyone out; he saved a mere four games. In August, the Angels released him. For all practical purposes, that ended his career. In 1989 the Kansas City Royals signed him to a minor league contract, but released him in June.

Knowing nothing but baseball, Moore did not know where next to turn. He had financial problems and marital difficulties of long standing; he was, when he drank, a wife beater. He seems always to have suffered from depression, and the unforgiving fans did not help matters. On July 18, 1989, he shot and wounded his wife three times and then turned the gun on himself. Psychologists, the secular clergy, maintain that "the pitch" had nothing to do with his suicide—it was being out of baseball, financial and marital problems. That may be so, but Moore was not Henderson, who later said "this is a game. It's not life and death." For Moore, it was.

Having made a near miraculous comeback, the 1986 Red Sox faced the New York Mets in the World Series, one remembered for another painful play and for another miraculous comeback—this time by the Mets. The Red Sox opened the series with two wins in New York's Shea Stadium, but the Mets fought back, winning the next two games in Boston. Game five, at Fenway, went to the Red Sox, who were then only one game away from their first world championship since 1918.

Boston led by two after the first two innings, but the Mets tied the score in the fifth. The Red Sox took a one-run lead in the seventh; the Mets tied it in the eighth. The score remained tied at the end of regulation play, but in the top of the tenth Dave Henderson led off with a home run and his teammates quickly added an insurance run—it was 5-3 in favor of the Red Sox going into the Mets' half of the inning. Ace reliever Calvin Schiraldi retired the first two Met hitters he faced—one more out and the Red Sox would be world champions. Future Hall of Famer Gary Carter, determined not to make the final out, kept the Mets alive with a single. Pinch-hitter Kevin Mitchell also singled, but Schiraldi went ahead of Ray Knight 0-2. The Red Sox were now only one *strike* away from victory.

Under enormous pressure, Knight, who would be voted series MVP, hit Schiraldi's next pitch for a single, scoring Carter and sending Mitchell to third; the score was now 5-4. Red Sox manager John McNamara quickly summoned Bob Stanley to pitch to outfielder Mookie Wilson. With the count 2-2 on Wilson, Stanley uncorked a wild pitch that allowed Mitchell to score the tying run and Knight to advance to second base. That took some of the pressure off Wilson, who fought Stanley on every pitch. On the Red Sox hurler's tenth offering, Wilson hit a slow grounder up the line toward first baseman Bill Buckner. "There is no way [Stanley] would have beat me to the bag," the Met player later insisted. He did not have the chance. "It gets through Buckner," television broadcaster Vin Scully shouted. "Here comes Knight, and the Mets win it!" They won game seven as well, 8-5.

Bill Buckner played 22 seasons for five major-league teams: Dodgers, Cubs, Red Sox, Angels, and Royals. He collected 2,715 hits and compiled a lifetime average of .289. In a Cub uniform in 1980, he won the National League batting title. He was an outstanding hitter, a good base runner (until an ankle injury slowed him), and a fine fielder. But the media, and too many so-called fans, never let him forget his error—not, at least, until the Red Sox won world championships in 2004 and 2007, thus breaking "the curse of the Bambino."

On an emotional opening day in 2008, Buckner walked from left field to the mound at Fenway Park and threw out the first ball of the new season. He had tears in his eyes as he received a standing ovation. At a press conference afterwards he said, "I really had to forgive, not the fans of Boston, per se, but I would have to say in my heart I had to forgive the media for what they put me and my family through. So, you know, I've done that and I'm over that." The burden that Bill Buckner carried for so long serves to remind us that memory should always leave room for forgiveness—what Paul Ricoeur called "reconciled memory." Some of baseball's most costly—or tragic—misplays have tested fans' ability and willingness to forgive.

Consider the case of catcher Mickey Owen, who played for the Cubs from 1949 to 1951. Sometime during those years, the union boss of the Wrigley Field grounds crew, whom my father knew, arranged to have me and my younger brother meet Cub players as they made their way down the ramp from the locker room to the diamond. Most of the players walked past us with little more than a nod or hello, but Owen stopped to talk, pleasantly and at length. He made a fuss over my brother and signed a ball for me. That experience is one of my fondest baseball memories.

Owen was what he seemed to me to be: a good and kindly man. He broke in with the Cardinals in 1937 and, during his four years in St. Louis, earned a reputation as a reliable defensive player and a respectable hitter, though one who possessed little power. After the 1940 season, the Cardinals traded him to Brooklyn, where he played during the war years. In his first year in a Dodger uniform he became famous, or rather infamous, for one miscue. The Dodgers won the National League pennant and prepared to face their crosstown rivals: the Yankees, led by Joe DiMaggio.

The Yankees won game one in Yankee Stadium, 3-2, but the Dodgers bounced back in game two, winning by the same score. The series moved to Brooklyn's Ebbets Field for game three, but the Yankees eked out a 2-1 victory. With pressure on them mounting, the Dodgers took a 4-3 lead into the ninth inning of game four. On the mound for the Bums was hard-drinking Hugh Casey, who later took his own life. He retired the first two men to face him. Only Tommy Henrich, a great clutch hitter, stood in the way of a Dodger victory that would even the series.

With the count on Henrich 3-2, Owen called for a curve ball. "It looked like a fast ball," the Yankee outfielder later recalled, "but when it broke it broke down so sharply that it was out of the strike zone. I committed myself too quickly. I tried to hold up but I wasn't able to." Home-plate umpire Larry Goetz signaled strike three, but the ball glanced off the heel of Owen's glove and rolled far enough away for Henrich to reach first base safely; it went into the record book as a passed ball. Casey would have to get a fourth out, but before he could do so, four Yankee runners crossed the plate. Stunned, the Dodgers failed to score in their half of the ninth, and the next day they dropped game five and the series, 3-1.

Owen, who had handled 476 consecutive chances without an error during the regular season, offered no excuse: "I should have had it, but it got away from me," he said. He feared the fans' wrath, but he was spared the kind of unforgiving treatment that Buckner was later to receive—and this tells us something about that earlier era. "I got about 4,000 wires and letters," he told

W. C. Heinz of the *Saturday Evening Post* on the 25th anniversary of the historic error. "I had offers of jobs and proposals of marriage. Some girls sent their pictures in bathing suits, and my wife tore them up." Nevertheless, he must have known how he would be remembered.

Jocko Conlan did not think of Owen primarily as the receiver who let an important pitch get away from him, but as an honest man. Sometime during the 1943 season, when he was calling balls and strikes for a Dodger game, Jocko became involved in a brouhaha that almost led to his resignation. George Barr, who was the third-base umpire for the contest, called a balk on the Bums' Johnny Allen. Allen was incensed, and so was Branch Rickey, who was in the stands. He saw Jocko shake his head in conversation with Owen and jumped to the conclusion that he was telling the catcher that Allen had been falsely charged. In fact, Jocko had merely indicated that he had not *seen* a balk.

That is what Jocko told Rickey, who then called him a liar. Jocko was irate and threatened to resign unless he received an apology. The following day he asked Owen to tell Rickey the truth, and the catcher immediately agreed to do so. Before the day's game, Jocko confronted Rickey, who expressed his regret: "I spoke to Owen," he said. "I was wrong. I apologize." The "old man," Jocko recalled in his memoirs, "was always a booster of mine after that. Just because I stood up for my rights, and because Mickey Owen told the truth."

After World War II, Owen involved himself in what baseball owners regarded as a challenge to the reserve clause. Along with a few others, including Sal Maglie, he accepted an offer from the wealthy Jorge Pasquel to play ball in Mexico. Commissioner A. B. "Happy" Chandler threatened to ban for life any player who "jumped" to the Mexican League, but Pasquel was offering tempting sums of money. By the time Owen began to have second thoughts, it was too late—major league baseball refused to take him back for three years. He did not play in the United States again until the Cubs signed him in 1949.

After the Cubs released him at the end of the 1951 season,

Owen played one more year, for the Red Sox in 1954, before re-
tiring. In his 13 seasons as a big leaguer he hit a respectable .255
and won recognition for his work behind the plate—the infamous
passed ball notwithstanding. In retirement he founded the
Mickey Owen Baseball School in Missouri and never complained
about his misfortune: "I would've been completely forgotten," he
said late in life, "if I hadn't missed that pitch."

When Owen died in 2005, the *New York Times* obituary linked
him in baseball lore with Ralph Branca, Bill Buckner—and Fred
Merkle. Merkle broke in with the New York Giants late in 1907
and went on to play 16 seasons in the major leagues. He compiled
a career batting average of .273 and played a fine first base, but
during the 1908 season he made a mistake that earned him the
permanent label "Bonehead."

The Giants led the National League by half a game when they
hosted the second-place Cubs at the Polo Grounds on September
23. Because their regular first baseman, Fred Tenney, was suffering from lumbago, Merkle, then only nineteen, started his first
major-league game.

The Giants came to bat in the bottom of the ninth with the
score knotted 1-1. With one out, Cub pitcher Jack Pfiester gave up
a single to Art Devlin, but then got Moose McCormick to hit into
a force out. Merkle then singled to right, sending McCormick to
third. That brought Al Bridwell, hitless in three trips, to the plate.
He singled to right-center, driving McCormick home with what
should have been the winning run; jubilant fans poured onto the
field. In an effort to escape the crush of a mob, Merkle headed for
the clubhouse—without bothering to touch second base. Cub second baseman Johnny Evers noticed this and managed, somehow,
to retrieve the ball—or *a* ball. As he touched second, he appealed
to umpire Hank O'Day, who called Merkle out.

According to a baseball rule, often ignored at the time, if the
third out is a force, any run scored is nullified. It being impossible
to resume play, the umpires declared the game a tie and, after con-
sidering many protests and objections, the National League Board

of Directors backed them up and scheduled a makeup game for October 8. That game proved to be decisive, because the Giants and Cubs finished the season with identical records of 98-55. When the Cubs won the game, and the pennant, 4-2, Merkle stood condemned for the "boner" that had necessitated a playoff. Nothing he did during the remainder of his career could erase the stain. Only when he returned to the Polo Grounds for Old-Timers' Day in 1950—again, a better time—did the crowd greet him with cheers, bringing tears to his eyes. "It makes a man feel good to hear such cheers after all these years," he said. A burden lifted at last.

Unlike Fred Merkle, Carl Mays was never to know forgiveness. A hard throwing "submarine" (that is, underhand) pitcher, Mays broke in with the Red Sox on April 15, 1915. In 1917, he won 22 games and lost only 9. The following year he went 21-13 and won two World Series games against the Cubs. And yet his personality was such that he made few, if any, friends among his teammates—"a man with a permanent toothache," one of them said. Players on other teams formed an even worse opinion of him, largely because he had a habit of hitting batters and throwing in the direction of their heads. On July 29, 1919, the Red Sox traded him to the Yankees, prompting novelist Howard Camerik to imagine that that trade, rather than the sale of Babe Ruth several months later, was the reason why the Red Sox fell under a curse.

Whether or not the Red Sox were cursed, Mays himself seems to have been. On August 16, 1920, he went to the mound against the Indians at the Polo Grounds, where the Yankees then played their home games. In the fifth inning, Cleveland shortstop Ray Chapman stepped into the batter's box. As Mays went into his windup, he noticed that Chapman had shifted his back foot, a sign that he was preparing to bunt. In an attempt to induce him to pop the ball up, the Yankee hurler threw the pitch up and in. Chapman seemed to freeze at the plate, and the ball struck him on the left temple. Hitters did not then wear protective helmets and doctors quickly determined that his brain had suffered extensive damage. Shortly after midnight, a team of surgeons operated, but without success; Chapman died at 4:40 a.m. on August 17. To add to the tragedy, his wife Kathleen took her own life in 1928, and the following year his daughter, Rae Marie, died of complications from the measles.

Because of his reputation as a headhunter, many believed that Mays intended to bean the popular Chapman. While he expressed his regret, the pitcher always protested his innocence. "It was an accident, nothing else," he said. "But what happened to me in August of 1920 is the only thing anybody remembers." The ball, he said, was wet and scuffed, making it difficult to control. And in any event, he, like most pitchers of his day, regarded brushback pitches as part of the game, a legitimate weapon in the war against hitters.

No one but Mays—and perhaps not even he—could know whether or not the beaning was intentional. But it cost him a place in the Hall of Fame. In a 15-year career, he won 207 games and lost only 126; his ERA was an impressive 2.92. "I think I belong," he said late in his life. "I know I earned it. Just look at my record. But just because I killed a man in an accident, they keep passing me up." The closest he came to Cooperstown was in 2008, when a special induction committee considered 10 players whose careers began before 1943. Mays received only three of the nine votes needed for admission to the Hall. Great was the loss on that August day in 1920.

In his novel *The Curse of Carl Mays*, Camerik makes passing mention of Tony Conigliaro, the late Red Sox outfielder. He did so in the knowledge that "Tony C" too was felled by a pitched ball. After joining the Red Sox in 1964, Conigliaro quickly established himself as one of the game's premier sluggers—and most eligible bachelors. But on August 18, 1967, tragedy struck. California Angels' pitcher Jack Hamilton hit him with a pitch that fractured his left cheekbone and severely damaged his left retina (he had dislodged his helmet in a desperate attempt to avoid being hit); it nearly cost him his life.

Conigliaro missed the entire 1968 season but made a miraculous comeback the following year. He belted 20 home runs and drove in 82. Even better in 1970, he smashed 36 homers and knocked in 116, but his vision began to deteriorate late in the season, and the Red Sox traded him to the Angels. Midway through a poor 1971 season, he knew that he could not see well enough to play and announced his retirement. He made a brief comeback attempt with Boston in 1975, but before the season was out he retired for good. Many observers had regarded him as a future Hall of Famer. In 1982 he suffered a massive heart attack and lapsed into a coma; he died on February 24, 1990.

And Hamilton? "I certainly wasn't throwing at him," he said. "I was just trying to get the ball over. Tony stands right on top of the plate. He hangs over the plate as much as anyone in the league." Red Sox shortstop Rico Petrocelli, who was in the on-deck circle when Conigliaro was struck, has testified to that truth. Although the hard-throwing right hander pitched creditably in 1968, he lost it in 1969—in part, one cannot help thinking, out of fear of hitting another batter. He retired from baseball before the season ended.

Pat McCarvill, the protagonist of Camerik's novel, is the forty-something mayor of Boston who wanted, more than anything in life, to be a major-league pitcher. Having given up his ambition after no more than a brief stint in the minors, he joins a senior-league team in an effort to recapture what might have been. Pitching in Yankee Stadium—the season is over for the Yankees—he is hit in the head by a line drive off the hitter's bat. It is an event that recalls the real-life tragedy of Herb Score. A left-handed pitcher, Score broke in with the Cleveland Indians in 1955. He went 16-10, posted a 2.85 ERA, and recorded 245 strikeouts, tops in the major leagues. That was good enough to win rookie of the year honors. In 1956, he was 20-9 with an ERA of 2.53; once again he was the strikeout leader with 263. No one doubted that he would one day take his place in the Hall of Fame.

On the night of May 7, 1957, Score went to the mound against the Yankees at Cleveland's Municipal Stadium. In the first inning, Yankee shortstop Gil McDougald hit a line shot that struck Score full in the face. Out of instinct, he fielded the ball with blood streaming from his right eye, nose, and mouth. He suffered a broken nose and hemorrhaging in the eye. McDougald was devastated and vowed to retire if Score lost his sight. He did not lose it, but he was never the same; over the next five years with the Indians and White Sox, he won a mere 17 games. He retired early in 1962 with a career record of 55-46. What might have been? Mickey Mantle called Score the greatest left-hander he ever faced. Indian great Bob Feller said he "would have been probably one of the greatest, if not the greatest, left-handed pitchers who ever lived. [He] had just as good a curveball as Koufax and a better fastball."

What might have been? That question has been asked of The Mick as well. How much more would he have accomplished with healthy legs? And it has been asked of a man whose natural ability some baseball men—including Leo Durocher—have compared to that of Mantle and Mays: Pete Reiser. In 1941, his first full year with the Dodgers, "Pistol Pete" led the National League in hitting (.343), runs (117), doubles (39), triples (17), and slugging (.558). He had lightning speed—the Dodgers clocked him at 9.8 for 100 yards in his baseball uniform and spikes. In 1946, he stole home eight times.

Reiser's fearless and aggressive play ruined his career and almost cost him his life. In a 1958 profile of the ill-fated outfielder, W. C. Heinz reported the gruesome details. In Reiser's two and a half years in the minor leagues, three seasons of Army ball, and ten years in the majors, he had to be carried off the field 11 times. Seven times he crashed into outfield walls. He was hitting .380 in 1942 when he ran at full speed into a concrete wall. Once, in 1946, the Dodgers' clubhouse doctor called for a priest, who administered the church's last rites. Often he played when he should have been in a hospital. When his injuries forced his retirement in 1952, he expressed no regrets. "God gave me those legs and the speed," he said, "and when they took me into the walls that's the way it had to be. I couldn't play any other way."

Players like Tony Conigliaro and Herb Score and Pete Reiser were anything but losers, but their personal tragedies constituted great losses to baseball. They remind us that the game is more about losing than winning. Chicago Cub fans need little reminding—though once, long ago, they did. In 1908, the Cubs faced the Detroit Tigers in the World Series, and for the second year in a row they won easily. They stood at the pinnacle of the baseball world; in contrast, the 1908 Yankees finished the season in the American League cellar, seventeen games out of seventh place. It was not the New Yorkers but the Cubs who were meant when anyone spoke of a diamond "dynasty."

The Chicago team was not always known as the "Cubs"; in 1876, it became a charter member of the National League of Professional Baseball Clubs as the Chicago White Stockings. Managed by Al Spalding, the White Stockings won the National League championship in that year. Cap Anson—Robert Frost's boyhood hero—then guided them to five more championships through 1889.

In 1890, the club became the Chicago Colts and suffered a decline, even though Anson remained at the helm. Perhaps the name brought with it bad luck, so they tried others, such as "Orphans," "Remnants," and "Spuds." None appealed, and during the 1900 season Charles Sensabaugh, sports editor of the *Chicago Daily News*, called the team the "Cubs," a name that began to catch on in 1902 but did not become official until 1907. It might be best to date the beginning of the "Cubs" to the arrival in 1898 of Californian Frank Chance, who was to become their "Peerless Leader" as manager and player. A catcher turned first baseman, Chance took over the field generalship from Frank Selee in 1905 and, between 1906 and 1910, led the Cubs to four National League pennants and two World Series victories.

Chance himself contributed to making the Cubs the best team in baseball, but so did the other members of what was to become the most famous double-play trio in baseball history (they entered the Hall of Fame as a unit): (Joe) Tinker to (Johnny) Evers to Chance. Rounding out an outstanding infield was third baseman Harry Steinfeldt. Chance's stellar pitching staff included Mordecai "Three-Finger" Brown, Ed Reulbach, and Jack Pfiester; catching them was the talented Johnny Kling. Chance and his men captured the pennant in 1906 by posting a record that has never been equaled: 116 wins and 36 losses. They were therefore heavy favorites to defeat their weak-hitting cross-town rivals, the White Sox, in the World Series. All the more disappointing, then, when they lost to the "Hitless Wonders" four games to two.

At the start of the 1907 season, Chance was still livid. "You're a fine bunch of stiffs," he told his charges. "Maybe you so-and-sos have learned your lesson in overconfidence, and what happens when you underrate the other so-and-sos." They had. They posted another impressive record, 107-45, and repeated as National League champions. In the World Series, they faced the Detroit Tigers and the young Ty Cobb; it was over quickly. After playing to a tie in game one, the Cubs swept the American Leaguers. In the World Series rematch of 1908, the Tigers managed to win only one game.

No one living at the close of the 1908 season would witness another Cub World Championship. No one could have predicted that the mighty Cubs would become famous, and for some strange reason loved, for being losers. There is no rational explanation; one can only recount what has happened. The Cubs had another fine season in 1909, winning 104 games and losing only 49, but that was not good enough to best the Pittsburgh Pirates for the pennant. The same number of wins gave them the pennant the following year, and they entered the World Series against Connie Mack's Philadelphia Athletics as heavy favorites. The A's pitching, however, proved too much for them—they lost the Series in five games.

Between 1911 and 1916, the Cubs sank ever lower in the National League standings: second, third, fourth, fifth. Managers came and went after owner Charles Murphy fired Chance before the 1913 season: Johnny Evers, Joe Tinker, even Hank O'Day, umpire for the "Merkle Game." Fred Mitchell, who had had a less than impressive record as a pitcher for several major league teams, took the reins in 1917; the Cubs finished no better than fifth place. In 1918, however, enough players were off to war to make it possible for the team to win the pennant, albeit in a curtailed season. Among their better players, in addition to the great Grover Cleveland Alexander, who went to war after winning two games, was—Fred Merkle.

The Cubs' opponents in the World Series were the Boston Red Sox, led by pitcher-outfielder Babe Ruth. The Babe beat the Cubs twice, and his team took the Series in six games. But for the North Siders—the Cubs moved from the West Side of the city in 1916— a new era was about to begin. Charles Weeghman, who made a fortune with a lunch counter chain, had purchased the franchise from Murphy and Charles Taft in 1916. The park into which he moved the Cubs that year had been home to the Chicago Whales, one of the teams in the short-lived Federal League.

Among Weeghman's partners was the chewing gum magnate, William Wrigley, Jr. Over the next five years, Weeghman's financial situation worsened, and he was obliged to borrow money from Wrigley, using Cub stock as collateral. Eventually he had to declare bankruptcy and Wrigley, already in control of much of the team stock, purchased enough from other owners to obtain complete control. Cubs Park became Wrigley Field. Knowing nothing about running a baseball team, Wrigley the business genius hired as president and general manager William Veeck, a sportswriter who knew little more. Their combined inexperience showed. The Cubs finished third in 1919 and 1928, but fourth, fifth, seventh, or eighth in the other seasons of the roaring twenties.

In 1926, however, Veeck played a hunch that paid off—he hired as manager Joe McCarthy, a career minor leaguer. It did not take McCarthy long to build a powerhouse. Heading into the 1929 season, the Cub roster included future Hall of Famers Hack Wilson and Kiki Cuyler (outfielders), Gabby Hartnett (catcher), and Rogers Hornsby (second baseman). They were joined by other outstanding players such as outfielder Riggs Stephenson, first baseman Charlie Grimm, and pitchers Charlie Root, Guy Bush, and Pat Malone.

Led by McCarthy, the 1929 Cubs won 98 games and lost only 54. They finished in first place, ten and a half games ahead of the second place Pirates, and went confidently into the World Series against the A's. The American Leaguers were, however, no slouches. They had three future Hall of Famers (four counting Mack): Jimmie Foxx, Al Simmons, and Mickey Cochrane. They had posted a regular season record of 104-46, good enough to finish 18 games ahead of the second-place Yankees.

To the surprise of almost everyone, Connie Mack chose Howard Ehmke as his starter for game one of the Series. Ehmke was a career .500 pitcher nearing the end of his playing days, but he convinced his manager that there was "one great game left in this old arm." Throwing nothing but junk, he struck out 13 Cubs and won the game 3-1. The teams split games two and three, the A's winning the second 9-3, the Cubs the third 3-1. It was game four in which the Cubs began to look as though they were under some kind of curse. They led 8-0 going into the last, the Philadelphia, half of the seventh inning.

"It was my intention at that stage of the game," Mack later recalled, "to send in substitutes for all the regulars at the start of the eighth inning. But when we came to bat in the seventh some odd things began happening." Indeed. Al Simmons led off with a home run and Jimmie Foxx followed with a single. Bing Miller also singled when Hack Wilson lost the ball in the sun. Before the Cubs knew it, the score was 8-4.

Growing uneasy, McCarthy lifted Charlie Root and called in lefty Art Nehf to pitch to the left-handed Mule Haas, who promptly lined one to center that Wilson again lost in the sun, allowing the batter and two base runners to score. Before the fire was finally put out, 10 A's had crossed the plate—the game ended in their favor, 10-8. Traumatized, the Cubs lost game five (attended by President Hoover), and the Series, 3-2. Two weeks after the Cubs' crash, the stock market followed suit. The Great Depression had begun.

Wrigley and Veeck held McCarthy responsible for the Cubs' failure and decided to find a new manager. Before they could act, however, McCarthy resigned near the end of the 1930 season and the Cubs, now led by Rogers Hornsby, finished second. What was more memorable was the performance of Hack Wilson, who hit a National League record 56 home runs; "broken" only by Mark McGwire, Sammy Sosa, and Barry Bonds, it still stands. Even more important, Wilson drove in 191 runs (not 190—based upon recent research), a record that has rarely been approached and will most likely never be broken. Unfortunately, Wilson was a drunk and after one boozy episode in August 1931, Hornsby suspended him for the rest of the season and then traded him to the Dodgers.

Hornsby had every right to regard Wilson as incorrigible, but he was never able to gain the confidence of his players. The Cubs finished third in 1931 and would not likely have done better in 1932 had Veeck not intervened. When he learned that Hornsby had borrowed money from his players to pay his gambling debts, he replaced him as manager with Charlie Grimm, the popular first baseman. Thanks to Grimm, good pitching, and the acquisition of former Yankee Mark Koenig, the Cubs won the pennant and prepared to meet the powerful Yankees—now managed by McCarthy, who was looking for vindication or revenge. He got both. The Yankees swept the Cubs.

William Wrigley died early in 1932, leaving the Cubs to his son, Philip K. Wrigley, who did not share his interest in the game. The younger Wrigley could not rely upon William Veeck for long because the latter went to his reward in the fall of 1933, a year in which the Cubs finished third. They did no better the following year, but in 1935 they again claimed the pennant, thanks to an astonishing 21-game winning streak in September. Gabby Hartnett was still around and led the team with a .344 average. A Chicago-born teenager by the name of Phil Cavarretta took over at first base and hit .275 while batting in 82 runs. The pitching staff was led by Lon Warneke, Bill Lee, Larry French, and Charlie Root.

Not a bad team, but not good enough to defeat the Tigers in the World Series. The men from the Motor City took the Series in six games, handing the Cubs their fifth Series defeat since the great victories of 1907 and 1908. In light of that unhappy string, perhaps it was just as well that they finished second in 1936 and 1937. Things looked even worse for them in 1938, until late July when Hartnett replaced Grimm as manager. After that they began to close in on the league-leading Pirates. In a crucial game against Pittsburgh, played on September 28, there occurred one of the most unforgettable moments in Cub history. The score was tied 5-5 in the bottom of the ninth—and darkness had set in.

Wrigley Field, by this time also known as "the Friendly Confines," did not have lights, and the game was of such importance that the home umpire—yes, it was Jocko—had decreed after the eighth inning: "We'll go nine, and that's it." Mace Brown, the Pirates' ace reliever was on the mound; he retired the first two Cub batters. That brought player-manager Hartnett to the plate. With the count 0-2, Brown tried to slip a slider past him, but Hartnett drove the ball into the first row of the bleachers in left—the "home run in the gloaming." The blow demoralized the Pirates and the Cubs went on to win the pennant. They again faced McCarthy's Yankees in the Series, and again they were defeated—swept; it was the Cubs' sixth Series' loss in a row.

The Cubs slipped to fourth place in 1939 and finished in the second division in 1940, 1941, 1942, and 1943. They climbed back to fourth in 1944, though their record was an unimpressive 75-79. Thanks to the fact that the powerful St. Louis Cardinals, winners of the 1942, 1943, and 1944 pennants, had lost several key players to the military draft, and thanks also to the acquisition, from the Yankees, of pitcher Hank Borowy, the Cubs won the 1945 pennant, their last such victory in the twentieth century. Just why the New Yorkers gave up on Borowy remains a mystery. Halfway through the 1945 season, he was 10-5 with an ERA of 3.13, slightly off his 1944 record of 17-12, 2.64, but still good. After joining the

Cubs in late July, he posted a record of 11-2 and an ERA of 2.13. The Chicagoans would not have won the pennant without him.

The Cubs' World Series opponents were the Detroit Tigers, who relied upon two outstanding pitchers—Hal Newhouser and Virgil "Fire" Trucks—and slugging outfielder Hank Greenberg. Trucks and Greenberg had only recently been released from active military duty. The Cubs had the better team. In addition to Borowy, the pitching staff was bolstered by Claude Passeau (17-9, 2.46 ERA) and Hank Wyse (22-10, 2.68 ERA). Their outfield was solid. In left was Harry "Peanuts" Lowrey, a steady player who had acted in films as a child; in 1952, he would play a role in *The Winning Team*, a film starring Ronald Reagan as Grover Cleveland Alexander. In center was Andy Pafko, who possessed a throwing arm it was inadvisable to challenge. In right was Bill "Swish" Nicholson.

Like most Cub fans my age or older, I remember Nicholson's big swings that often failed to meet the ball—hence his nickname. Although he had had an off year in 1945, he had been wartime baseball's greatest slugger. In 1943 and 1944 he led the National League in home runs and RBIs. In a double header at the Polo Grounds on July 23, 1944, he hit four consecutive home runs. When he next came to the plate, Giants' manager Mel Ott ordered him to be intentionally walked—with the bases loaded.

In the infield, the double-play combination of Lennie Merullo and Don Johnson was good, but the men at the corners were Cub all-time greats: third baseman and lead-off man Stan Hack, a .323 hitter on the season; and first baseman Phil Cavarretta, who hit .355, won the batting title, and was named the National League's MVP. Mickey Livingston handled the catching duties well, and he had three backups.

The Cubs should have prevailed. Of course, they did not. Borowy shut out the Tigers 9-0 in game one, played in Detroit's Briggs Stadium, but the Tigers took game two behind Virgil Trucks, 4-1. In game three, Passeau pitched what until then was the finest game in World Series history, taming the Tigers 3-0 on one hit, a single by Rudy York. Game four was the first played in

Wrigley Field, and the Tigers won it 4-1 behind Dizzy Trout, whose son Steve later pitched for the Cubs. But that was not the worst of it—the Cubs came under a curse.

William Sianis, owner of the Billy Goat Tavern, had two tickets to the game. He came to Wrigley with his beloved goat Murphy and was allowed in. But sometime in inning four, P. K. Wrigley ordered the goat ejected because, as he told Sianis, "the goat stinks." "The Cubs," Sianis replied, "ain't gonna win no more. The Cubs will never win a World Series so long as the goat is not allowed in Wrigley Field." When the Cubs lost the Series, Sianis wrote to Wrigley: "Who stinks now?"

Say what you will, the team has never even made it to a World Series since 1945. Misfortune has dogged the Cubs in ways that are difficult to explain without reference to the Curse of the Billy Goat. In 1994, out of desperation, the team even formally welcomed Sianis's son and a goat to the ballpark. Too little, too late, apparently.

Hal Newhouser, whom the Cubs had hit hard in game one, pitched the Tigers to an 8-4 victory in game five; Borowy started and lost the game. With their backs to the wall, the Cubs notched a 12-inning 8-7 victory in game six; Borowy pitched the final four innings and got the win. For the deciding game seven, Grimm handed the ball to—Hank Borowy, who did not survive the first inning. The Tigers went on to win the game, and series, 9-3 behind Newhouser.

Why, one wonders, did Grimm call upon an overworked Borowy to pitch game seven? The right-hander had thrown a shutout in game one, pitched five innings in game five, and four in game six. He was exhausted. It was all the more disheartening because securing the former Yankee had been one of the very few moves in which Cub General Manager Jim Gallagher could take pride. Hired by Wrigley in 1940, Gallagher was, like Veeck, a newspaper man—*Chicago Herald-American*—with little knowledge of the game, but he shared his employer's determination to keep players' salaries as low as possible and his conviction that "Beautiful Wrigley Field" would keep the fans coming, no matter how poorly the team performed. (Jim Brosnan, a onetime Cub pitcher, said of Wrigley: "His slogan was Come Out and Have a Picnic, and the other teams usually did.")

When Gallagher retired from baseball, he settled in Port Republic, Virginia, near my home. I spent a long afternoon with him one summer day in 1988 and found him to be something of a curmudgeon. After reading a review I had written of a book about John McGraw, he complained because I had failed to mention the fact that the "Little Napoleon" managed the National League in the first All-Star game. Okay. Still, after some coaxing he was willing to speak of his career. He reminded me, among other things, of the fact that Wrigley had been willing—however reluctantly—to install lights in Wrigley Field during World War II, but the necessary material was needed for the war effort.

Inexperience seems to account for the fact that Gallagher was often hoodwinked by rival general managers. He sent Billy Herman, a future Hall of Famer, to the Dodgers in return for Johnny Hudson, Jimmy Gilbert, and $65,000; released outfielder Augie Galan, who went on to have several outstanding years with the Dodgers; and sold the terrible-tempered Russ "Mad Monk" Meyer, who then helped the Phillies and Dodgers win pennants. He seemed to believe that, having won the 1945 pennant, the club could stand pat. The Cubs managed to finish a respectable third in 1946, but they were a poor sixth the following year and ended in the cellar in 1948.

The '48 team may have been the worst in the franchise's history—it was certainly a portent of what lay in the future. The team did have Eddie Waitkus at first and Andy Pafko at third, but shortstop Roy Smalley, Sr., hit a meager .216 and committed 34 errors. No Joe Tinker, he had a tendency to throw the ball into the visitor's dugout. Smalley taught the young George Will, and doubtless many others, "why this is called a vale of tears." Second baseman Hank Schenz is worth mentioning only because he later helped the 1951 Giants set up the sign-stealing system that may have tipped off Bobby Thomson.

Schenz's backup was Emil Verban, who according to Will is

"a patron saint of Cub fans because he symbolizes mediocrity under pressure." "I didn't think I was a mediocre ball player," a hurt Verban protested. He was right to do so. Why pick on a man who hit .280 in a Cub uniform (his obscurity? the sound of his name? the fact that he had only one career home run?)? Others might better serve as a "symbol." Clyde McCullough was a good catcher with a strong arm, but a weak hitter (.249 as a Cub). Center fielder Hal Jeffcoat also had a strong arm but could not hit major league pitching (.248 lifetime), so in 1954 he moved to the mound, where he performed only slightly better (39-37 lifetime, ERA 4.22). To be sure, the '48 Cub pitching staff could have used him. In the last year before the Cubs traded him to the Phillies, Hank Borowy went 5-10. Dutch McCall found a variety of ways to lose 13 games in a row—1948 was his only year in the majors. Ralph "String Bean" Hamner was 5-9 (6-13 in his Cub career). Warren Hacker was at the beginning of his uninspiring career (62-89 lifetime).

The 1948 Cubs did, however, have Bert Wilson, a radio announcer who could stir excitement, even when the team was losing—which was the majority of the time. Routine fly balls off Cub bats were, on Wilson's telling, near home runs. A single promised to ignite a Cub rally. Things were never hopeless. Before the advent of television, a fan could either go to Wrigley Field or listen to Wilson report the game on the radio. "I don't care who wins, as long as it's the Cubs," he would say.

Those who remember radio days know a great truth: listening was better than viewing a game. "Radio," David Halberstam wrote, "made the games and the players seem vastly more important, mythic even." Moreover, you could do other things as you listened—work, pretend to pay attention in class, drive, rest your eyes. More important, you could use your imagination—see the action in your mind, what Roger Angell has called "the interior stadium."

By his own account, imagination is exactly what the young Ronald Reagan needed when he broadcast Cub games on WHO in Des Moines, Iowa, during the 1930s. Reagan never actually witnessed the games in Wrigley Field; a telegrapher sent a report after each pitch and each play of the game. An operator in Des Moines decoded the bare bones Morse reports for Reagan, who then had to make up the details of play. This was a challenge, but it helped that the future president knew the game well.

Radio broadcasts of games continued, of course, but by the early 1950s, television had become the medium of choice, and Jack Brickhouse the voice of the Cubs. He had a more difficult job of maintaining enthusiasm, but somehow he always managed to soldier on. Like so many others, I will never forget his home run call (for Cub hitters): "Hey, Hey!" Poor Jack. Never, from 1949 to 1966, did the Cubs escape the second division, not once. They finished fifth three times, sixth once, seventh seven times, eighth five times, ninth once, and tenth once.

Were there any "bright spots" during that long stretch? Yes. Hank Sauer was one. The Cubs obtained him in 1949 and he quickly became "the mayor of Wrigley Field." In 1952, he led the team to what for it was an impressive .500 season, a feat for which he was named the National League's MVP. His supporting cast was not good enough to produce a winning team, but at least Cub fans could enjoy the slugging outfielder's tremendous home runs.

In the late 1940s and early 1950s, the Cubs could always count on an overflow crowd when the Dodgers came to town. Black Chicagoans came in droves to root for Jackie Robinson, Roy Campanella, and Don Newcombe. Not until late in 1953 could they, or any Chicagoans, cheer black Cubs. But then they struck gold, in the persons of Gene Baker and Ernie Banks. Baker was a solid performer at second base and played with the team until traded to Pittsburgh in 1957. Banks played his entire Hall of Fame career in Chicago and earned the sobriquet "Mr. Cub."

"My teammates," Banks recalled years later, "didn't make a fuss about me being there—the first black to play for the Cubs. The press made the fuss. It was a bigger issue to them than it was to us. Fans always ask me how it felt to be the first black to play for the Cubs. I always say, 'No big deal. The guys were nice; they treated me well. No big deal.' People have a hard time believing that, but it's true."

For those of us who endured years of rooting for a losing team, Banks was a gift from heaven. A fine shortstop (and later first baseman), he was a born hitter. Though slender of build, he had remarkable wrists, and almost all of his 512 home runs were line shots. But there was more to Banks than his athletic ability. He was an eternal optimist ("let's play two," he was famous for saying) who gave us hope in dark times, a good man who played the game with a lowly team and never complained, never gave anything but his best, and never thought it his responsibility to lecture Americans concerning racial matters.

"I don't think," Banks has said, that "it's up to black athletes to get involved in political or racial issues. Our main objective should be to play whichever sports we are involved in and play well.... It is not [an athlete's] duty to comment on things outside of his game or to bum-rap somebody else in airing his personal feelings. It is important to be yourself, be a man, accept things as a man." To have watched this gifted man play was a privilege for which all of us Cub fans remain grateful.

Banks always said that he learned to play—and, more important, to love—the game from Buck O'Neil, who managed him when he played for the Kansas City Monarchs of the Negro Leagues. O'Neil was himself a good player, probably good enough to have played in the Majors had the game been open to black men. He did make it to the Cubs in 1962, as the first black coach in Major League history. For many years, he scouted for the Cubs; Lou Brock was one of his discoveries. In 1998, as a scout for the Kansas City Royals, he was named Midwest Scout of the Year.

Late in life, O'Neil gained unexpected celebrity when he appeared in the Ken Burns television series on baseball. What struck anyone who watched the series was not only the man's personal charm but the complete absence of bitterness. "Why would you feel sorry for me," he asked at one point. When baseball writer Joe Posnanski, who spent months traveling with him around the country, asked, as he often did, "How do you keep from being bitter?" O'Neil's answer was always the same: "Where does bitterness take you? To a broken heart? To an early grave? When I die I want to die from natural causes. Not from hate eating me up from the inside." Buck O'Neil lived into his nineties, and as an ambassador of good will he brought joy to a great many people.

He certainly brought joy to the Cubs when he convinced a young Billy Williams not to give up the game and return to his Whistler, Alabama, home. The Sweet-Swinging Williams became the greatest left-handed hitter in the team's history and fashioned a Hall of Fame career. He and others, like Ron Santo, who came along toward the end of the 1950s, gave us something about which to cheer. It is also true, however, that happy memories of the 1950s Cubs revolve around the beauty of Wrigley Field, the voices of public address announcer Pat Pieper and hot dog vendor Gravel Gertie, the thrill of seeing great players on visiting teams, and the pleasures of living during one of the best times in our nation's history (about which more in due course). To appropriate Wordsworth, bliss was it in that time to be alive, "but to be young was very heaven!"

This, despite the fact that the 1950s Cubs were the property of P. K. Wrigley, who did not want to draw upon money from his chewing gum empire. Baseball, he insisted, must pay for itself. As a result, he paid his players as little as possible. "We didn't make any money playing," Hank Sauer recalled. "In five years, my biggest raise was when I got to be MVP in '52. I got up to $37,500." Andy Pafko never made more than $35,000. Many other players registered similar laments. They had reason to, but it should also be noted that even then they made far more than an average American worker.

Wrigley also had a habit of changing managers at the drop of a hat. He once fired Phil Cavarretta during spring training! But his worst idea was the infamous College of Coaches, a system that lasted for two years, 1961 and 1962. Why bother with a manager who would probably not last long anyway? Instead, Wrigley decreed that there would be eight coaches who would take turns as "head coach"; among the original contingent were such luminaries as Elvin Tappe, Vedie Himsl, Harry Craft, and Bobby Adams. Under the direction of the College, the 1961 Cubs compiled a 64-90 record, finishing seventh. The following year they won 59 games and lost 103, the worst record in team history. That was poor enough for ninth place in the expanded league. Fortunately, the freshly minted New York Mets were even worse. They went 40-120.

Wid Matthews, who replaced Jim Gallagher as general manager in 1950, was not exactly a master of the art of trading, either. It was he who, in 1951, traded Pafko and three other players to the Dodgers for catcher Bruce Edwards, pitcher "Lefty" Joe Hatten, outfielder Gene Hermanski, and infielder Eddie Miksis. "Miksis will fix us," the Cub executive predicted. Not so, alas. In his six years in a Cub uniform, Miksis batted .243 and could not always be trusted to throw the ball from second to first. In his two years in Chicago, Hatten went 6-10, with an ERA of 5.51. Edwards hit .235 in three seasons; Hermanski .258 in three. Pafko contributed to four pennant-winning efforts in Brooklyn and Milwaukee.

Not to be outdone by Gallagher and Matthews, John Holland (general manager, 1957–75) pulled off the worst trade in Cub, perhaps in major league, history. In June 1964, he sent the gifted Lou Brock to St. Louis for pitcher Ernie Broglio. Brock went on to a storied Hall of Fame career. In his two and a half years as a Cub, Broglio, who had compiled an 18-8 record for the Cardinals in 1963 (ERA 2.99), won 7 games and lost 19 (ERA 5.40). Thus did he join many other Cubs in the Hall of Infame. What Cub fan can forget Bob Speake, for example? A rookie in 1955, Speake had an April-May that made him look like Ted Williams. He hit .304, belted 10 home runs, and batted in 31 runs; he was on fire. But then National League pitchers found his weakness—up and in, as I recall. At season's end, his average was .218; he had a total of 12 home runs and 43 RBIs. June through September had not been kind to Mr. Speake.

One of the players who went to the Dodgers with Pafko was

Wayne "Twig" Terwilliger, a second baseman who could play any infield position. For the Cubs (1949–51), Twig hit only .232, but on the other hand he was a mediocre fielder. (It is only fair to add, however, that he was still managing—successfully—in the minor leagues at age 80!) Outfielder-third baseman Carmen Mauro (1948–51) hit at a .219 clip, not good enough to give opposing pitchers nightmares. Better, however, than the .189 average that catcher Carl Sawatski compiled in 1948–50 and 1953.

Kevin "Chuck" Connors played for the Cubs in 1951; he hit 239. Prior to that he had played in one game for the Dodgers in 1949. He came to bat but once, and I remember his telling what happened. "I grounded into a double play," he said, "but I hit the ball so hard that the next day I batted cleanup—in Montreal!" Connors was a better basketball player—he played briefly for the Celtics—but he was still better as the actor who fashioned a long screen career, including the starring role in the hit TV show *The Rifleman*.

Not all of the 1950s Cubs were losers, but pitching is the name of the game, and the Cubs never had it. This, in fact, is the key to understanding their history of losing. Johnny Schmitz, who also went to Brooklyn in the Pafko trade, had his moments; he went 18-13 with the last-place 1948 club. Bob Rush wasn't so bad; he won 17 and lost 13 in 1952 and could look very good on occasion. But neither Schmitz nor Rush was a true standout. Lefthander Paul Minner (1950–56) was 14-9 in 1952, but a career (with the Cubs) 62-79 pitcher.

Most Cub hurlers were worse. Calvin Coolidge Julius Caesar Tusckahoma McLish (1949, 1951): 5-11 ("he can pitch with both hands and not too well with either"—Robert L. Burnes). Johnny Klippstein (1950–54): 31-51. Walt "Monk" Dubiel (1949–52): 14-21. "Bubba" Church (1953–55): 5-8. "Moe" Drabowsky (1956–60): 32-41. Dick Drott (1957–61): 24-34. Glen Hobbie (1957–64): 61-79. Dick Ellsworth (1958, 1960–66): 84-110. Jim Brosnan (1954, 1956–58): 14-18.

Of Brosnan, however, there is more to be said. In 1958, the Cubs traded him to the Cardinals. He took it hard. "The Cubs traded me down the river to St. Louis just six months after I'd bought a home in suburban Morton Grove. This dastardly and underhanded maneuver (the first time is always the most painful) fulfilled a hoary maxim in baseball: buy a home in the town in which you play, and you'll be traded before your first lawn blows away." After donning a Cardinal uniform, he pitched in 33 games, winning eight and losing four. More important, his friendship with Robert Boyle of *Sports Illustrated* opened the door to the writing life for which he seems to have been born. Always something of an intellectual—he was an avid reader of serious books—Brosnan ruminated about the life he was living, that of a major-league ballplayer.

Not only did Boyle invite Brosnan to write for *SI*, he introduced him to an editor at Harper & Brothers, who told the pitcher that he might be interested in an inside book about life in the big leagues. Throughout the 1959 season, one that he divided between the Cardinals and the Cincinnati Reds, Brosnan kept a diary that he published as *The Long Season*. The book quickly became a classic not only because Brosnan wrote it himself, but because it offered readers a glimpse of players as they were, humans rather than heroes. They checked out women in the stands (and elsewhere), grumbled about their poor pay, mocked their managers, worried about their futures, and drank—some, like Brosnan, more than others.

Brosnan was blessed with a fine ear for the way players talked, and he could turn a phrase. His wit was sharp, cynical, self-deprecating. He was almost painfully honest about his limitations as an athlete and his failures on the mound. But this is only another way of saying that, like all good writers, he was more self-aware than most people. He was also, despite his hard-drinking, tobacco-chewing, irreverent persona, a sensitive man. Boos and fan insults wounded him, and so did Cardinal manager Solly Hemus's obvious—at least to Brosnan—hostility.

It was therefore with a sense of relief that he received word, in the middle of the "long season," that the Cardinals had traded him to the Reds. "The second time you're sold you don't feel a thing." There is reason to doubt this. In his book, he reported that his wife, upon learning that he had been swapped for outfielder-turned-pitcher Hal Jeffcoat, cried "couldn't they get more for you than that? Oh, honey, they just wanted to get rid of you."

In 20 games for the 1959 Cardinals, Brosnan compiled a record of 1-3. In 26 games for the Reds, managed by Mayo Smith and, before the season was out, by Brosnan favorite Fred Hutchinson, he won eight and lost three. More important, his ERA dropped from 4.91 (Cardinals) to 3.35 (Reds). A pitcher's ability, he wrote in *The Long Season*, "is best reflected in his Earned Run Average. From experience professionals come to realize that a good pitcher will have a good E.R.A.; conversely, a pitcher whose E.R.A. is consistently under 3.50 gains a reputation of being a pretty good pitcher."

Despite pretty good pitching by Brosnan, the Reds finished the 1959 season in fifth place with a record of 74-80. According to the pitcher/writer, however, they had nothing of which to be ashamed. "Every baseball season is just long enough for each player to do something to which he can look back with satisfaction. On the last day of the season those are the moments you want to remember, and probably those are the memories that make you a little sad."

In 1960, the year *The Long Season* appeared, Brosnan pitched in 57 games for the sixth place (67-87) Reds. He won seven games, lost two, and saved 12; his ERA was an impressive 2.36. Encouraged by the success of his first book, he decided to write one about the 1961 season. He titled it *Pennant Race* because, to the surprise of many, the Reds won the National League championship, and Brosnan played a major role in their success. He went 10-4 and saved 16; his ERA was again impressive—3.04. It was his finest year on the mound, but his happiness was not complete. "There are varying degrees of disappointment in the life of a ballplayer," he wrote in the introduction to *Pennant Race*, "for even on a pennant winner he must lose 35 percent of the time."

The book takes the reader through another season, and the story is much the same—perhaps that is why, as Brosnan conceded, the book, though worth reading, lacks the original power of *The Long Season*. Both books are well written, insightful, and cynically witty. Brosnan revealed what one might call the *prose* of the game, or what the players were like as men—warts and all. But he showed us little or nothing of the game's poetry, the unforgettable on-field achievements of players who, whatever their personal foibles and failures, continue to inspire us. We may regret the fact that Babe Ruth and Mickey Mantle drank too much and chased women, but that is not why we remember them.

The Reds lost the 1961 World Series to the Yankees of Mantle and Maris four games to one. Brosnan pitched a total of six innings in three games and posted a terrible ERA of 7.50. He had a good season in 1962, though his won-lost record was only 4-4. He saved 13 games and posted a 3.34 ERA. In 1963, the last of his nine years in the majors, he pitched in only six games for the Reds before being traded to the White Sox, for whom he went 3-8 with 14 saves; his ERA was an excellent 2.84. His career record was 55-47 with 67 saves and an ERA of 3.54; not too bad for a writer, one who possessed a long memory of good times and bad. In *The Long Season,* for example, he reported the "first thing I look for in the morning paper. Did the Cubs lose? Since they were the first team ever to trade me I get a vicarious thrill out of seeing them get beat." His has been a thrilling life indeed!

It is a wonder that the Cubs did not attempt to regain the aging Brosnan after he made a success in Cincinnati. They often acquired star players who had passed their prime, but unlike castoffs who joined the Yankees—like Johnny Mize and Enos Slaughter—these did not discover new life in the Friendly Confines. Ralph Kiner gave them a couple of decent years (1953–54), but he was not the hitter he once was—and he was very slow afoot. With Kiner in left and Hank Sauer in right, center fielder Frankie Baumholtz (a very good hitter) had acres to cover; the story, probably apocryphal, has it that he once caught a ball in foul territory! The great Monte Irvin joined the Cubs in 1956 and had a respectable year, but it was the last of his Hall of Fame career. Alvin Dark, who loved Wrigley Field, played for the Cubs in 1958–59. He did well enough, but he too was near the end of his excellent career. During those same years, Bobby Thomson—*the* Bobby Thomson—also played for the team. He also played reasonably well for a man whose diamond days were all but over.

P. K. Wrigley stepped out of character in 1966 when he hired Leo Durocher to manage the Cubs. "This ain't no eighth-place ballclub," the Lip declared, and he was right. The Cubs finished tenth (last) that year, but in one of their few brilliant trades they acquired Ferguson Jenkins from the Phillies. In 1967, the right hander compiled a 20-13 record, the first of six straight 20-win seasons. The ace of the staff and future Hall of Famer was joined by left-hander Ken Holtzman and right-hander Bill Hands. For once, the team had a first-class starting rotation. They finished third in 1967, and again in 1968.

In 1969, the Cubs looked like world beaters. Dick Selma joined an already stellar pitching staff and the infield was composed of All Stars: Ron Santo at third, Don Kessinger at short, Glenn Beckert at second, and Ernie Banks at first. Billy Williams patrolled left field, Jim Hickman played in right; center fielder Don Young was the only weak link in the starting lineup. Randy Hundley did the catching. "In '69," Santo recalled, "everybody had that feeling that this was it." The Cubs won 11 of their first 12 games and were 16-7 at the end of April. They went 16-9 in May and 17-11 in June. In July, they slowed to 15-14 and the first sign of trouble appeared on the horizon. Against the Mets on July 8, Young failed to catch two fly balls and cost the team the ballgame.

Some of the players had begun to find Durocher hard to take and were particularly irritated by his criticism of Banks; "he's too old to play the game anymore," Leo declared when he arrived in Chicago. More important, the tough manager never gave his starters a day of rest and, as the season progressed, they began to show clear signs of fatigue. "We were tired," Fergie Jenkins recalled. "Leo played the regulars almost the whole season."

Still more important, the Mets were truly amazing. Led by

pitchers Tom Seaver and Jerry Koosman, the New York club came from 8 ½ games back on August 13 to finish 8 games ahead of the Cubs, who went 9-17 in September. The Curse of the Billy Goat— or the Curse of the Black Cat? On September 9, the Cubs were in New York for a crucial series with the Mets. Someone released a black cat onto the playing field and, after prowling past Ron Santo, who was standing in the on-deck circle, the cat stared menacingly into the Cub dugout. Naturally, the Cubs lost the game— and whatever heart was left in them.

The Durocher-led Cubs finished second in 1970 and third in 1971, but relations between manager and players continued to sour. The team had a record of 46-44 in 1972, when Wrigley fired Leo the Lip. Whitey Lockman took over and the Cubs finished a distant second to the Pirates. Over the ensuing four seasons, the Cubs reverted to form; they did not come close to .500. Then, on April 12, 1977, Wrigley died, leaving the club to his son William, who cared even less about the game. He watched with little interest as his team continued to distinguish itself by its lack of distinction, and on June 16, 1981, he sold it to the Chicago Tribune Company.

Before the 1982 season, Tribune officials hired Dallas Green, who had guided the Phillies to a world championship in 1980, as Cub general manager. Determined to produce a winner in a hurry, Green became an active trader. He sent shortstop Ivan DeJesus to Philadelphia for veteran shortstop Larry Bowa and, as a throw-in, second baseman Ryne Sandberg, who went on to a Hall of Fame career. Later he traded for Dodger third baseman Ron Cey and Phillies outfielders Gary Matthews and Bob Dernier. And then, on June 14, 1984, he succeeded in acquiring pitcher Rick Sutcliffe from the Indians.

Sutcliffe posted a 16-1 record and helped the Cubs win the National League East, their first championship of any kind since 1945. Cub fans everywhere were euphoric. But the Cubs had not yet won the pennant. To do so, they would have to defeat the San Diego Padres in the National League Championship Series (NLCS), then a best-of-five affair. With Sutcliffe on the mound, they won the opener in Wrigley 13-0, then captured game two 4-2; they needed only one victory in three games in San Diego. They lost the first, but still led the series 2-1. Game four was tied 5-5 in the Padres's half of the ninth. With a runner on base, Steve Garvey came to the plate and hit a Lee Smith offering out of the park. The series headed for the deciding game.

Sutcliffe (who would win the Cy Young Award) returned to the mound and enjoyed a 3-0 lead through five innings. In the sixth, the Padres narrowed the gap to one run. In the seventh, with one out and a San Diego runner on second, Tim Flannery hit a snake-like ground ball that found its way through the legs of Cub first baseman Leon Durham, eerily prefiguring ex-Cub Bill Buckner's error in the 1986 World Series. The runner on second scored, and before the inning ended three more runners had crossed the plate. The Padres won the game—and the series—6-3.

In 1989, the Cubs again won the National League East; they faced the San Francisco Giants in the NLCS, which was now best of seven. The most memorable thing about that series was the magnificent hitting duel between rival first basemen Will Clark of the Giants and Mark Grace of the Cubs. Clark went 13 for 20 for a .650 average; Grace 11 for 17 for a .647 average. Unfortunately, there was little else for Cub fans to cheer—the Giants won four of five. Still no pennant.

In 1998, the Cubs were the wild card entry in the National League Division Series (NLDS), first played in 1995 after the creation of three divisions in 1993 (the 1994 playoffs having been called off because of a player strike). In the best-of-five series the Atlanta Braves swept the Cubs. In 2003, the Cubs gained a measure of revenge. Having won the National League Central Division title, they defeated the Braves 3-2 in the NLDS. They then faced the Florida Marlins in the NLCS.

The Cubs lost game one and then won three in a row before losing game five. Game six, played in Wrigley Field, was crucial. Behind the fine pitching of Mark Prior, the Cubs took a 3-0 lead into the eighth inning. Prior retired the first batter, and the Cubs were five outs away from their first World Series appearance since

1945. But the next Marlin batter, Juan Pierre, doubled. In a long at bat, Luis Castillo hit a fly ball that drifted foul toward the seats along the left field line. The second out was almost in the Cubs' grasp. Left fielder Moises Alou reached into the stands and, just as he was about to snag the fly, Cub fan Steve Bartman, instinctively grabbing for the ball, deflected it away.

Prior then walked Castillo. Ivan Rodriguez singled. Miguel Cabrera grounded to short, but the usually sure-handed Alex Gonzalez booted it. Before the Cubs could get out of the inning, eight runs had scored, and the Marlins went on to an 8-3 victory. Unable to recover from the shock, the Cubs lost the decisive game seven, 9-6. It seemed that the curse had not yet been removed. Not until 2007 did the Cubs have another opportunity; new manager Lou Pinella guided them to the National League Division Series—but the Arizona Diamondbacks swept them in the NLDS.

Pinella led his charges to another Division championship in 2008—and then watched as Manny Ramirez and the Dodgers inflicted another sweep on his charges. When it came to the big prizes, they were still "loveable losers." But hope springs eternal. On October 27, 2009, the Chicago Tribune Company sold the Cubs to Tom Ricketts and the Ricketts family, whose wealth comes from Ameritrade, the online discount broker. Will new ownership lift the curse? I may be forgiven for remaining skeptical.

"Everyday baseball," Roger Angell has written, "is stuffed with failure and defeat, overflowing with it, and for most of us who have followed the game over a distance, losing more and more appears to outweigh the other outcome as the years slip by, and at the same time deepens our appreciation of the pastime." Cub fans know whereof he speaks, but so do all fans. Of his 1953 Dodgers, who won the pennant but lost the World Series to the Yankees, Roger Kahn wrote this in *The Boys of Summer*: "Losing after great striving is the story of man, who was born to sorrow, whose sweetest songs tell of saddest thought, and who, if he is a hero, does nothing in life as becomingly as leaving it. A whole country was stirred by the high deeds and thwarted longings of The Duke, Preacher, Pee Wee, Skoonj [Carl Furillo] and the rest. The team was awesomely good and yet defeated. Their skills lifted everyman's spirit and their defeat joined them with everyman's existence, a national team, with a country in thrall, irresistible and unable to beat the Yankees."

Even the greatest teams, such as the '53 Dodgers, fail to win championships more often than they win them. In their best years, the greatest hitters—Rogers Hornsby, Ted Williams—failed to hit safely 60 percent of the time. "The thrill of victory, the agony of defeat, the cliché has it, but my guess," Joseph Epstein has observed, "is that for those who have undergone both, the memory of defeat in sports is stronger and sharper." This is true, and for good reason. Life too, as Kahn suggested, is primarily about losing: losing parents and other loved ones, friends, jobs, health, memory—life itself. Such losses are painful, but like losses in sports, they teach the valuable lesson of human limitation and shed light on the meaning of life and the paradoxical words of Christ (St. Matthew 16: 25): "For whosoever will save his life shall lose it: and whosoever will lose his life for my sake shall find it."

The Fifties

IN HIS DEBATE WITH GEORGE WILL, DONALD KAGAN ARGUED CONVINC-
ingly that the decade of the 1950s was baseball's golden age. Even
Will, promoter of the more recent game, seems to recognize this.
In a piece titled "Fifties Baseball: Not Long on Nuance," he conceded that the decade had the two most famous pitching performances in baseball history—Don Larsen's perfect World Series
game and Harvey Haddix's twelve perfect innings. Moreover, he
wrote, the decade included baseball's most storied home run
(Bobby Thomson's) and most famous catch (Willie Mays's).

"One Way," the conflicted pundit continued, "to gauge the
caliber of baseball in a decade is to pick an All-Star team from
those who played a significant portion of their careers in it."
These were his fifties' selections: Catchers: Roy Campanella, Yogi
Berra; First Basemen: Stan Musial, Ted Kluszewski; Second Base-
men: Jackie Robinson, Nellie Fox; Third Basemen: Eddie Math-
ews, Ken Boyer, George Kell, Al Rosen; Shortstops: Ernie Banks,
Luis Aparicio, Phil Rizzuto, Pee Wee Reese; Outfielders: Ted
Williams, Willie Mays, Mickey Mantle, Duke Snider, Frank Robin-
son, Henry Aaron, Richie Ashburn, Al Kaline; Pitchers: Warren
Spahn, Whitey Ford, Robin Roberts, Bob Lemon, Early Wynn.
One is tempted to say: "case closed."

A further concession by Will cements the case for fifties baseball: "The best and most profound mark made on baseball by the
fifties was the inclusion of black players, without whose subsequent participation baseball would have been a pale shadow of
itself." The color barrier came down later in some places than in
others—the Phillies had no black players until 1957, the Tigers

until 1958, the Red Sox until 1959—but come down it did, to the considerable benefit of game and country. The list of memorable black players of the 1950s is long and distinguished: Willie Mays; Monte Irvin; Ernie Banks; Henry Aaron, a hitter so consistent that he eventually caught and passed Babe Ruth in career home runs; Frank Robinson, a terrifying—to pitchers—line drive hitter; Larry Doby, the Cleveland standout; Satchel Paige, the ageless wonder. Each of them found his rightful place in baseball's Hall of Fame.

The breaking of the color line also opened the door for outstanding black players from Latin America, the first of whom was Cuba's Orestes "Minnie" Minoso, signed by the Indians in 1948. Minoso's best years were those with the Chicago White Sox, 1951-57, when he hit over .300 five times (he finished with a career average of .298). But statistics tell only part of the story. He was an exciting player to watch—at the plate (he was hit by pitches 192 times), in the field (he was a three-time Gold Glove winner), and on the base paths (he stole 205 bases).

In 1955, while Minnie was patrolling left field for the White Sox, Puerto Rico's Roberto Clemente joined the Pittsburgh Pirates. It was the beginning of an 18-year Hall of Fame career that ended tragically when a plane carrying him and humanitarian relief to earthquake victims in Nicaragua crashed. An outstanding hitter, he compiled a career batting average of .317. He won four National League batting championships and collected 3,000 career hits. As a right fielder he had no equal. He won 12 Gold Glove Awards; only Mays had as many. His arm was so strong and accurate that few were willing to run on it. By almost universal consensus, he was the greatest defensive right fielder in the game's history.

Clemente was League MVP in 1966 and World Series MVP in 1971, when he batted .414. For him, Major League Baseball waived the five-year period before a player is eligible for the Hall of Fame; he won election within months of his death, the first Latin American player to be honored. President George W. Bush awarded him the Presidential Medal of Freedom posthumously in 2002. He was, in short, one of the game's immortals.

In addition to the great black players and those who made Will's All-Star list, the '50s gave us Vic Raschi, Allie Reynolds, Eddie Lopat, Bob Feller, Carl Erskine, Joe Page, Gil Hodges, Carl Furillo, Johnny Mize, Enos "Country" Slaughter. More, too, should be said of Stan "The Man" Musial. The Cardinal out-fielder-first baseman was one of the game's greatest hitters—as great, in my opinion, as Ted Williams. Unlike Williams, Musial could and did hit to all fields. In 22 seasons, he batted .331, collected 3,630 hits, and belted 475 home runs. Hitting out of his distinctive crouch, he had no known weakness. "I never gave him the same pitch twice in succession," Warren Spahn testified. "I didn't dare." Dodger hurler Preacher Roe offered this sage advice to his fellow pitchers: "throw four wide ones and try to pick him off first."

I happened to be in Wrigley Field on April 18, 1954, a day in which the Cardinals were in town to play the Cubs. For years I had told friends what I witnessed that afternoon—in the mistaken belief that I alone remembered it. But I have now learned from a Joe Posnanski piece in *Sports Illustrated* that the story is often told, for the light it sheds on Musial as a man and a baseball great.

With lefty Paul Minner on the mound for the Cubs, a Cardinal runner on first, and one out, Musial stepped to the plate. He drove a double—or what appeared to be a double—down the line in right (I thought it was a home run but my memory was otherwise perfect). When the first base umpire called the ball foul, the Cardinals, especially manager Eddie Stanky, went crazy; but Musial returned to home plate and leaned on his bat without uttering so much as a word of protest. When order was finally restored, he stepped back in the box and hit a fair ball in exactly the same spot in right!

Many of the players mentioned thus far in this chapter wore New York uniforms—Yankee, Giant, or Dodger. New York was the capital of baseball in the 1950s; its three teams dominated the two leagues. And yet, as Kagan pointed out, fifties baseball was never boring. The Yankees and Dodgers almost always faced competition. In 1950, Philadelphia's young "Whiz Kids" won the National League pennant by defeating the Dodgers on the final day of the season. And we know what happened to the Bums the following year, the year of Thomson's home run. The Red Sox lost the 1949 pennant to the Yankees—also on the final day of the season.

In 1954, the Indians won 111 games and captured the American League pennant. Their Hall of Fame manager was Al Lopez, who, three years later, moved to Chicago to manage the White Sox; in 1959, forty years after the Black Sox scandal, he led the South Siders into the World Series. While Cub fans suffered through yet another losing season (74-80, fifth place), the "Go-Go" Sox stirred the Windy City, and, what was exceptional in the fifties, they did so with very little power. Catcher Sherm Lollar belted 22 home runs and outfielder Al Smith hit 17, but no other Sox player posed a long-ball threat.

What the team did have was pitching, defense, and speed on the bases. Future Hall of Famer Early Wynn had posted a 23-11 record for Lopez's 1954 Indians, but in December 1957, believing the right hander to be washed up, the Tribe had traded him to Chicago. That was a mistake. In 1959, Wynn went 22-10, good enough to win the Cy Young Award. Because he was so fiercely competitive, someone once asked if he would throw at his own mother. "I would if she were crowding the plate," he snapped back.

Billy Pierce, the winningest left-hander in White Sox history, had an off year in 1959 (14-15), but young Bob Shaw picked up the slack. Benefiting from Wynn's tutelage, Shaw had a career year, winning 18, losing 6, and posting a 2.69 ERA. Lopez could also rely on two ace relievers: Gerry Staley and Turk Lown. Staley posted an 8-5 record with an ERA of 2.24; he saved 14 games. Lown went 9-2 with an ERA of 2.89; he saved 15 games. Not surprisingly, he came into his own after the Cubs, for whom he toiled ineffectively from 1951 to 1958, gave up on him.

The Go-Go White Sox were particularly strong up the middle. At shortstop was future Hall of Famer Luis Aparicio of Venezuela;

in my opinion, and that of many others, no one has ever played the position better. He had incredible range and possessed a strong and accurate arm; he won nine Gold Gloves. Moreover, he was a steady performer at the plate. Teamed with Aparicio was second baseman, and future Hall of Famer, Nellie Fox. An excellent contact hitter, Fox struck out only 216 times in over 10,000 career appearances at the plate. In 1959, he batted .306—and .383 with runners in scoring position. In the field he led the league in putouts, assists, and fielding average. The American League honored him with its MVP award.

The Go-Go White Sox finished the season with a pennant-winning record of 94-60, five games ahead of the Indians and 15 games ahead of the Yankees. They faced the Los Angeles Dodgers in the World Series. The teams played game one in Comiskey Park, where Chicago writer and Sox fan Nelson Algren was in attendance. "Someone flew Tony Martin from Hollywood to sing the national anthem," Algren wrote in the *Chicago Sun-Times*. "Before he'd finished the Sox had scored twice." With Wynn and Staley pitching, the Sox coasted to an 11-0 victory. Ted Kluszewski ("Big Klu"), a late August acquisition, drove in five runs with a pair of two-run homers and a run-scoring single.

Nat (King) Cole sang the national anthem before game two, also played in Comiskey. The Sox's Bob Shaw took the mound against Dodger ace Johnny Podres. The Sox jumped to a 2-0 lead in the first inning, but the Dodgers' Charlie Neal made it 2-1 with a home run in the fifth. Algren, again covering the game for the *Sun-Times*, smiled to himself when Dodger manager Walter Alston pulled Podres, who was getting stronger by the inning, for a pinch-hitter in the seventh. "Another reason I felt the Dodger management was making a big mistake was because the pinch-hitter was somebody named Aram Puntformacion or something: an Armenian football player who may or may not be a cousin of William Saroyan's."

Algren was joking—punt formation. But the hitter was of Armenian descent and he did play on Stanford's 1952 Rose Bowl team. His name was Chuck Essegian, and he promptly drove the ball out of the park. Jim Gilliam followed with a walk and Neal hit his second homer. The Sox picked up a run in the eighth but fell short, 4-3.

The series then moved to Los Angeles's Memorial Coliseum, where the Dodgers captured the next two games, 3-1 and 5-4. Things looked grim for the Chicago boys, but they managed to prolong the series by winning game five 1-0 behind the fine pitching of Shaw, Pierce, and Dick Donovan. Back in Comiskey Park for game six, Wynn took the mound against Podres. Algren watched as the Dodgers scored two in the third and six in the fourth. "Wynn still looked like a twenty-game winner to me; between line drives." And yet: "I was still for Wynn, I was still for Fox; I was still for Big Klu. Because Los Angeles has always impressed me as being a city wired only loosely to reality. Furthermore, I've never been able to take football seriously and Armenians have always seemed implausible to me."

He may have been implausible, but with the score 8-3 in the ninth Essegian hit another pinch home run and the Dodgers took the series. It would be 46 years before the White Sox won another pennant. In 2005, they won the World Series by sweeping the Houston Astros.

The *Los Angeles* Dodgers went on to win eight more pennants and four more world championships, but they have never appealed in the way the *Brooklyn* Dodgers did. There was something compelling about the Brooklyn team of the late 1940s and 1950s, perhaps the fact that they were notable winners *and* lovable losers. The modern history of the team—it had won pennants and lost the ensuing World Series in 1916 and 1920—began in 1941, when it won the National League pennant, but lost the World Series to the Yankees in five games. It was in game four of that Series that Mickey Owen dropped a critical third strike.

In 1947, the Dodgers again won the pennant, and again they lost the World Series to the Yankees. Dodger fans did, however, receive two consolation prizes. In game four of the Series, Yankee hurler Bill Bevens (7-13 on the year) was one out away from pitching a no-hitter when pinch-hitter Cookie Lavagetto lined a double to the wall in right center that drove home two runs and gave the Dodgers a 3-2 victory. In game six, Dodger outfielder Al Gionfriddo, in for defensive purposes, robbed Joe DiMaggio of a home run with a remarkable catch at the fence in left—in a rare display of emotion, the Yankee Clipper kicked the dirt as he approached second base.

Once again, in 1949 the Dodgers won the pennant and lost the World Series to the Yankees in five games. The 1950 pennant went to the Whiz Kids of Philadelphia and the 1951 pennant to the Giants of Bobby Thomson, but in 1952, the Dodgers won again, only to lose the World Series to the Yankees in seven games. In the seventh inning of the decisive game, Yankee second baseman Billy Martin made a game-saving catch of a pop fly off the bat of Jackie Robinson.

Two men were out and the bases were loaded with Dodgers when Robinson hit what should have been an easy out. But neither Yankee pitcher Bob Kuzava nor first baseman Joe Collins, who had lost the ball in the sun, made a move toward the spot between the mound and first base toward which the descending sphere was headed. Seeing that his teammates were frozen in place, Martin made a mad dash from his position around second base; as Dodger runners were rounding the bases, he caught the ball a few inches from the ground. "I had nightmares for two or three months," Collins said later. "I can see that ball dropping and losing the World Series."

"Wait Till Next Year" was all that Dodger fans could say. In 1953, the Dodgers had what many considered to be their finest ball club. Roger Kahn, who covered that year's club for the *Herald Tribune*, had this to say in *The Boys of Summer*: "The Dodgers of 1953—not the pitching staff but the eight men in the field—can be put forth as the most gifted baseball team that has yet played in the tide of times."

No doubt that is why Jocko Conlan presented me with another treasure: a ball—"Natl League 1953"—autographed by Manager Chuck Dressen and Dodger players Billy Loes, Bob

Milliken, Billy Cox, Duke Snider, Pee Wee Reese, Joe Black, Roy Campanella, Carl Furillo, Wayne Belardi, Don Thompson, George Shuba, Dick Williams, Johnny Podres, Bob Morgan, Gil Hodges, Carl Erskine, Jim Gilliam, Russ Meyer, Jackie Robinson, Preacher Roe, and Cookie Lavagetto (coach). As we have seen, that club won another pennant but yet again lost the World Series to the Yankees; the irrepressible Billy Martin collected twelve hits for the winners. The one bright spot for the Bums came in game three, which they won 3-2. Winning pitcher Carl Erskine set a Series record by striking out 14 batters.

Dodger fans were understandably prepared for the worst when their boys won the 1955 pennant and—of course—found themselves confronted once more with their arch rivals, the Yankees. And things did look bad as the Bronx Bombers won game one 6-5 and game two 4-2, both at Yankee Stadium. The Series then moved to Ebbets Field, where the Dodgers, behind the fine pitching of Johnny Podres (on his 23rd birthday), beat the Yankees 8-3. Suddenly inspired, the Bums won games four (8-5) and five (5-3) in their home park. Down but not out, the Yankees won game six in Yankee Stadium, 5-1. The Series and the season had come down to one game. The Dodgers sent Podres back to the mound, and he pitched a beauty, shutting the Yankees out 2-0 on five hits. The Brooklyn Dodgers had won their first (and as it turned out, their only) World Championship—"This Is Next Year" the *Daily News* headline proudly proclaimed.

It had not been easy, even with Podres's superb effort. In the sixth inning, the Yankees had two men on base and no outs when the always-dangerous Berra came to the plate. Dodger manager Walter Alston had that very inning sent Sandy Amoros out to play left field in place of Jim Gilliam, who had moved to second base because Don Zimmer had been lifted for a pinch hitter. With the outfield around to the right, the left-handed Berra lined a pitch down the left-field line. Amoros, who was left-handed, made an outstanding running catch near the line, then turned and fired the ball to Reese, who relayed it to Hodges at first in time to double up Gil McDougald. "Lucky, lucky, I'm so lucky," said the modest Amoros.

The Yankees never threatened again. When Elston Howard, the Yankees' first black player, grounded to Reese to end the game, broadcaster Vin Scully spoke these famous words: "Ladies and gentlemen, the Brooklyn Dodgers are the champions of the world." It was a game that Dodger fans, indeed baseball fans, will never forget. Near the end of his life (he died in early 2008), Podres explained why to journalist and Dodger fan Thomas Oliphant. "One thing you have to keep in mind is what happened that day can never happen again. There will be other great seventh games, already have been. Someday someone will pitch another perfect game in the Series, someone will make another unassisted triple play, someone will hit another home run to win it all in extra innings. But the Brooklyn Dodgers will never win another championship. They are gone. The events of that day are frozen forever." "Frozen forever" and yet a moment that belongs to the '50s. Like Bobby Thomson's home run, the Dodger triumph was an example of what T. S. Eliot meant when he spoke of the "sense of the timeless as well as of the temporal and of the timeless and of the temporal together."

Referring to the 1940s and 1950s, the historian Doris Kearns Goodwin has written that "never would there be a better time to be a Dodger fan." Boys, even if they lived far from New York, had reason to agree—especially if, like me, they devoured the novels of John R. Tunis. Born in Boston in 1889, Tunis was educated at Harvard and studied law at Boston University. He served in France during the Great War, an experience that provided him with material for his fiction. After the war, he worked as a sportswriter for the *New York Evening Post* and as a tennis commentator for NBC radio, but he made his reputation as the author of a series of sports—particularly baseball—books for boys.

Or so they have always been regarded. He himself once said that he "continued writing these so-called boys' books, but I've never considered them that." Joseph Epstein, who along with Philip Roth and Stephen King is a Tunis devotee, thinks that may have been the secret of his success: there was "an absolute absence of condescension in [his books'] composition." Epstein recognized something else about Tunis: he used his baseball stories to teach moral lessons. At their best, Tunis knew, sports improved character by instilling discipline and a willingness to make sacrifices for the good of the team. As something of an athlete himself—he was a member of Harvard's tennis team—he learned "how to accept defeat, a lesson most Americans hate to accept, although defeat comes to us all in the end and we had better be ready for it."

I remember reading two of Tunis's baseball novels, both of which involve fictional Brooklyn Dodgers. *The Kid Comes Back* (1946) opens in World War II Europe. Having been drafted in 1941, Dodger center fielder Roy Tucker is the tail gunner on a plane sent over occupied France to bring supplies to the French Resistance. When the plane is forced to make a belly landing, Tucker suffers a painful back injury. He and his comrades are hidden by the Maquis, and Tunis offers some moral instruction. The French Resisters, women as well as men, serve as examples of courage and self-sacrifice. The Americans hear "of women who journeyed for miles by bicycle in mid-winter storms with messages." And so they did. The French wives of two ex-GIs who worked for my father in the late 1940s carried messages for the Resistance in their bicycle handlebars—at the risk of their lives.

But Roy learns another lesson in France: he should have taken his high school study of French more seriously. Education "meant living things, tools that were to be used later on in life. If you didn't have them, well, it was too bad for you, that's all." On their way out of France, he and his comrades are taken prisoner by the Germans, then rescued by the Resistance. Back home Roy undergoes treatment for his back and returns to the Dodger lineup, only to find that he fears re-injury. The rest of the novel revolves around his struggle with that fear, which, because of his character and indomitable spirit he eventually vanquishes.

Right: Jocko Conlan,
Hall of Fame umpire.

Below: Joe DiMaggio
after hitting safely in
45 straight games –
on his way to 56.

All photographs in
this section of the
book are courtesy of
the National Baseball
Hall of Fame Library,
Cooperstown, NY.

Left: Larry Doby, the American League's first black player.

Below: Mickey Mantle, baseball's greatest "natural."

Above: Roger
Maris, still the
legitimate
single-season
home run king.

Left: Andy
Pafko in the
late forties.

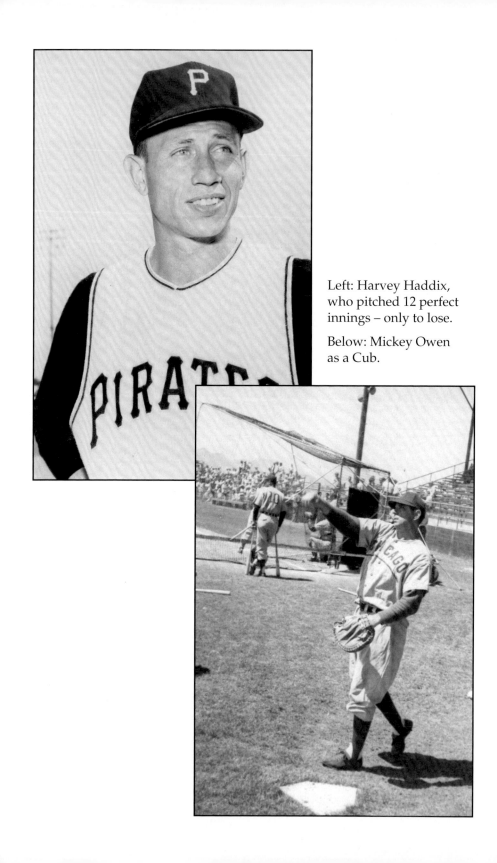

Left: Harvey Haddix, who pitched 12 perfect innings – only to lose.

Below: Mickey Owen as a Cub.

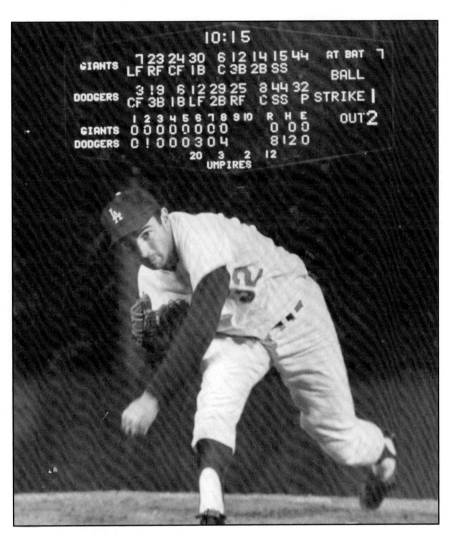
Sandy Koufax, the greatest pitcher of his time.

Left: Jim Brosnan, the pitcher as writer.

Below: Ted Williams, the game's greatest hitter?

Stan Musial and Mickey Mantle – diamond immortals.

Bob Gibson – intimidating.

In *Highpockets*, Tunis tells the story of another Dodger player, rookie right-fielder Cecil "Highpockets" McDade, modeled in part on Ted Williams. Highpockets is a left-handed slugger who hits for average but thinks of nothing but his personal statistics—the needs of the team never cross his mind. Because he is a pull hitter, the opposing teams place everyone except their third basemen on the right side of the infield—exactly like the famous "Ted Williams shift" designed by the Indians' Lou Boudreau in 1946. Like Williams, Highpockets refuses to hit into the vacated space on the left side of the diamond because he would have to sacrifice some of his power. "They pay off on the long ball in the majors," he tells his manager, who replies that his time in the majors may be brief if he continues to refuse to hit them where they ain't and to think only of himself.

Highpockets' attitude begins to change only when he runs over a boy who jumps in front of his car. In some of his most moving writing, Tunis tells a story of a seriously injured boy and a selfish ballplayer. Eager to befriend the boy, Highpockets is shocked to find that he has no interest in baseball; his passion is for stamp collecting. Highpockets educates himself in the ways of stamp collecting in the recognition that "there's no easy way to a boy's heart. Like everything else, you have to work for it." He is brought up short, too, when the boy's doctor tells him that he must act as part of the team—family, doctor, nurses—working to save the boy's leg, and perhaps his life.

Slowly Highpockets and the boy forge a friendship, each coming in time to share the other's interest. Out of this experience, the Dodger slugger learns to think of others and to understand the importance of team play; he begins to drive the ball to left and to subordinate his personal ambitions to the team goal of working together for victory. In this way, Tunis sought to teach young people that life, like baseball, ought to be about something other than winning at all costs, especially the cost of one's character.

John R. Tunis found inspiration in the Brooklyn Dodgers of the 1940s and 1950s—never, he knew, was there a better time to be a Dodger fan. Never, in fact, has there been a better time to be a baseball fan. There were just eight teams in each league, for a total of sixteen—since that time, fourteen teams have been added, as follows:

1961 – Washington Senators (now Texas Rangers)
      – Los Angeles Angels (now Los Angeles Angels of Anaheim)
1962 – Houston Colt .45s (now Houston Astros)
      – New York Mets
1969 – Montreal Expos (now Washington Nationals)
      – San Diego Padres
      – Kansas City Royals
      – Seattle Pilots (now Milwaukee Brewers)
1977 – Seattle Mariners
      – Toronto Blue Jays
1993 – Colorado Rockies
      – Florida Marlins
1998 – Arizona Diamondbacks
      – Tampa Bay Devil Rays (now Tampa Bay Rays)

Keeping track of sixteen teams posed little difficulty, but checking the progress, or regress, of thirty teams requires effort. And there is another problem with expansion: there is not enough major league talent to go around, at least not by fifties' standards. Competition for authentic major leaguers is keen and this fact, along with free agency, means that players bounce from one team to another. Before their career is over, many of them play for eight or nine clubs. It hardly needs to be pointed out that this has destroyed team continuity. The team that reports to spring training may bear little resemblance to the team that closed out the prior season. "I think," Ralph Branca has said, "that they [the players] change teams so often that sometimes you're rooting for a uniform and not a team."

In the fifties, things were different; "the extraordinary continuity of the lineup over the years . . . intensified our loyalty," Doris Kearns Goodwin observed. It is difficult to be loyal when a team can have wildly different lineups with each new season. One year a player is our sworn enemy, the next he is our first baseman! Second baseman Glenn Beckert, who played for the Cubs from 1965 to 1973, has testified to the importance of continuity to the ballplayers themselves. "I think when we played there was a lot more team concept. There was no free agency and guys stuck together. You knew who was on the Pittsburgh Pirates, St. Louis. Now, one or two guys stay there five or seven years. I think that's one of the good points of the game when I played."

There was no free agency because of the reserve clause that, prior to the 1970s, bound a player to a team unless traded, sold, or released. This, of course, made it possible for owners to pay players what they wanted to pay—which was not what a free market in talent would offer. Players were not particularly happy about low salaries, and yet many of them favored the clause in the interest of franchise stability. That began to change on October 7, 1969, when the Cardinals dealt their outstanding center fielder, Curt Flood, to the Phillies. Flood, who was then earning $90,000 a year, refused to report to the city of brotherly love, arguing that the reserve clause was a form of slavery; "a well-paid slave," he told Howard Cosell, "is nonetheless a slave." Coming from a black man at the height of the civil rights movement, the words carried weight.

Flood eventually took his case to the Supreme Court, where a 5-3 decision went against him. But the die had been cast. After the 1975 season, the Dodgers' Andy Messersmith and the Orioles' Dave McNally, both of whom had played the year without a contract, maintained that they were free agents. The case went to arbitration and arbitrator Peter Seitz ruled in their favor. For all practical purposes, that marked the end of the reserve clause, and as Phillies general manager Paul Richards put it, "the end of baseball as we know it." It was not long before players began their club hopping. They also began to demand, and to receive, multimillion-dollar salaries. Such incomes are the result of market decisions, and no one can fault men for being ever on the lookout for a better offer, but monster contracts inevitably shift their focus from winning to individual statistics. Almost every player is now an unreconstructed Highpockets.

In baseball, the importance of continuity cannot be exaggerated. Writing of "the decline of the national pastime," G. Edward White cites, in addition to free agency, the movement of teams from city to city. In search of more fans, greater seating capacity, and better media markets—in other words, larger profits—owners have done much to destroy the kind of civic identity that so endeared the *Brooklyn* Dodgers to their fans and to historians of the game (you have only to type in "Brooklyn Dodgers" at amazon.com for proof). By the time the Dodgers and Giants moved to the West Coast (1958), the Braves had already abandoned Boston for Milwaukee.

The fictional Brady Greer in Robert Booth's offbeat novel *The Perfect Pafko* came of age in Milwaukee during the fifties, "the happiest decade of the last half-century, the years between the end of the Korean War and the Kennedy assassination." It was certainly the happiest decade for the city's baseball enthusiasts. Losing money in Boston, where the Braves could not compete with the Red Sox for fan loyalty, owner Lou Perini moved his team to the nation's beer capital at the start of the 1953 season. Half a century had gone by since the last major league team, the Baltimore Orioles, had relocated (to New York).

Milwaukee fans greeted the Braves with open arms and hearts. "I don't think any city has ever gone as crazy over a baseball team," third baseman Eddie Mathews said years later. County Stadium drew 1,826,397 of the faithful that first year and the Braves rewarded them with a record of 92-62, good enough for second place in the Senior Circuit. Manager Charlie Grimm's lineup boasted such star players as Mathews, shortstop Johnny Logan, center fielder Billy Bruton, first baseman Joe Adcock, and catcher Del Crandall; in 1954, outfielder Henry Aaron began his Hall of Fame career. Until the 1960s, according to Mathews, "our lineup had been pretty much the same, very consistent."

And so had the starting rotation of Warren Spahn, Lou

Burdette, and Bob Buhl. According to the inimitable Stan Musial, Spahn was "the best pitcher and one of the great athletes of my era." During a Hall of Fame career that spanned 21 seasons, "Spahnie" won 363 games, more than any other left-hander in Major League history; and he would have added substantially to that total had he not lost three years while serving in World War II (he won a Purple Heart and a Bronze Star). He was a 20-game winner thirteen times, hurled two no-hitters, and posted a career ERA of 3.09. No one who was privileged to see him play will ever forget his high kick and smooth delivery.

The Braves dropped to third in 1954 but finished second in 1955 and 1956, the year in which Fred Haney took over as manager. Nineteen-fifty-seven was the year in which everything seemed to go right for the Braves, including their decision, in July, to call up Bob "Hurricane" Hazle from their Wichita farm club. "I don't know what happens to suddenly make a minor league ballplayer into Babe Ruth," Eddie Mathews puzzled, "but Hazle was right out of 'The Twilight Zone.' We were hanging in there pretty well before he arrived, but he just picked us up." In 134 at bats, Hazle hit a blistering .403, helping the Braves finish in first place, eight games ahead of the second-place Cardinals.

It was on to the World Series against Casey Stengel's Yankees. Behind the pitching of Whitey Ford, the Bronx Bombers won game one in New York, 3-1, but Lou Burdette, who had once been Yankee property, went the distance in game two, picking up a 4-2 win. The Series then moved to Milwaukee, where in game three Don Larsen, working in relief, won a 12-3 decision. Warren Spahn, the losing pitcher in game one, took a 4-1 lead into the ninth inning of game four, only to give up a game-tying homer to Elston Howard. The Yankees scored again in the top of the tenth, but the Braves fought back in their half of the inning. Johnny Logan batted in the tying run ahead of Mathews's two-run blast off Bob Grim.

Haney sent Burdette back to the mound in game five and the fidgety right-hander (Haney once said that "Lou would make coffee nervous") shut the Yankees out 1-0 on seven hits. Back in

Yankee Stadium, the home team, behind Bob Turley, forced a seventh game by winning 3-2. Spahn was scheduled to face Larsen in game seven, but when he came down with the flu, Haney gambled that Burdette could pitch on two days' rest. In one of the great pitching performances of the twentieth century, Lou again shut out the Yankees on seven hits. That made it three victories in seven days against an awesome New York squad.

The Braves repeated as National League champions in 1958, but their attendance dipped under 2,000,000 for the first time since 1953. Once again they faced the Yankees in the World Series. After winning three of the first four games, they became overconfident. "Maybe," Hank Aaron later reflected, "it was just that we expected the same magic all over again and that was impossible, because 1957 was a once-in-a-lifetime experience." The Yankees won the next three games, and the Series.

The following year, 1959, the Braves tied the Dodgers for the pennant but lost the playoff series—and attendance declined to 1,749,112. In 1960, the team finished second to the Pirates, who went on to defeat the Yankees in the World Series when Mazeroski hit his famous walk-off home run in game seven. Attendance slipped again, and it was becoming clear that Milwaukee fans were losing their enthusiasm for their one-time heroes. In 1962, Perini sold the club to a group of Chicago businessmen, headed by William Bartholomay. The new owners soon resolved to leave Milwaukee for Atlanta, and in an atmosphere of growing civic hostility they did so at the close of the 1965 season.

In *The Perfect Pafko*, protagonist Brady Greer "hates" the greedy owners and players for moving to Atlanta. But he retains warm memories of Andy Pafko, who played for the team from 1953 to 1959 ("How lucky can a guy get?" asked the Boyceville, Wisconsin, native when he learned that the Dodgers had traded him to Milwaukee). "That clean-cut, hard-working image of Andy Pafko had taken root in Brady's mind a half-century ago and now blossomed more with every story of a contemporary player's wife beating, drug rehab, or illegitimate kids. The happiest times Brady had spent with his father were while watching

Handy Andy and the Milwaukee Braves." In 1952, Topps, the bubblegum and baseball-card company, selected Pafko, then still with the Dodgers, to be on its #1 card. Whenever Greer looked at that card, it triggered memories of his youth, his father, and of a better time in America.

Inspired by the Braves' great initial success in Milwaukee, the St. Louis Browns packed their bags for Baltimore in 1954. The following year, the Philadelphia Athletics—memories of the Connie Mack era having faded—moved to Kansas City. Not good enough; in 1968, the team moved on to Oakland. As if all of this were not disorienting enough, try to follow this: the Washington Senators moved to Minneapolis, a city granted an expansion team, in 1961—they were then, and now, the Minnesota Twins. The "expansion" team became the new Washington Senators; but that team moved to Texas in 1972, where it metamorphosed into the Texas Rangers. One of the reasons why the Cubs maintain such an emotional grip on their fans—and on many baseball fans whose loyalty lies elsewhere—is that they have remained in Chicago and in Wrigley Field.

The Cubs' having remained in Wrigley is even more important than their having stayed put in the Windy City. In *Remembering*, Edward S. Casey wrote of the "elective affinity between memory and place. Not only is each suited to the other; each calls for the other." That is the reason, he says, we so "often seek out 'old haunts'" like the town and home in which we grew up or the school we attended ("homecoming"). For us Cub fans, a return visit to the "Friendly Confines" summons memories of earlier periods in our lives—times with our fathers or with our friends. "Loyalty and memory," Michael Kimmelman has written, "are what fill stadiums year in and year out."

The "place" on the North Side has changed incredibly little since 1937, when the bleachers were expanded and raised to their present height, the giant hand-operated scoreboard was installed in center field, and Boston ivy and bittersweet were planted at the base of the outfield wall (the ivy later overtook the bittersweet). There have, of course, been some changes; against the will of the fans, for example, the Tribune Company installed lights in 1988. The Good Lord was obviously displeased; the first night game, August 8, 1988, was rained out after four innings. In 1989 the owners expended money to construct private boxes on the mezzanine level originally occupied by the press box and broadcasting booths. In 2003 and 2005, they added seats. But the beautiful park remains almost completely free of advertising and has not been renamed for some commercial entity—the ultimate vulgarity.

So much baseball history has been made in Wrigley Field, history that cannot be transferred elsewhere. Our shared memories of Hack Wilson, Gabby Hartnett, Charlie Grimm, Hank Borowy, Andy Pafko, Hank Sauer, Ernie Banks, Billy Williams, Ron Santo, Fergie Jenkins, and numerous great players from visiting teams are closely tied to Wrigley Field, to that place on Chicago's North Side. Were the Cubs to move to another ballpark, even in Chicago, they could create new memories. But those memories would not be joined to those attached to Wrigley; place and memory are inextricably intertwined.

After—or for Bostonians before—Wrigley Field, the most beloved ballpark is Fenway Park. Perhaps its greatest charm is its age. Built in a drained but still rather swampy area of Boston called "The Fens," the park has been home to the Red Sox since 1912; it is the oldest park in use. When Tom Yawkey bought the Red Sox in 1933, he spent more than $1.5 million to reconstruct the park. By opening day 1934, Fenway's seating capacity had jumped from 27,642 to 33,817. More important, the park boasted a new 37-foot-high wall in left field; originally made of concrete and tin-covered wood (and since 1976 of hard plastic), it was covered with advertisements and at its base was (and still is) a hand-operated scoreboard. In 1947, the advertisements were removed and the wall was painted a dark green; the now famous "Green Monster" had been christened.

The Green Monster is certainly Fenway Park's most famous idiosyncrasy, but like all of its quirks—such as its angles—it is authentic because it was necessary to offset the short distance (310 feet) down the left field line. Quirkiness for the sake of quirkiness would not have appealed, precisely because it would have been the result of a plan. And "plans," when it comes to ballparks— even the retro Camden Yards—or to life, usually do more harm than good (cf. the Soviets' Five-Year Plans).

For the relentlessly rational mind, of course, planning is all. Hence, during the late 1990s the Red Sox's owners, led by John Harrington, floated the idea of building a new, planned park near where Fenway stands. The state and city pledged millions of dollars, but they quickly found themselves confronted by fierce opposition, led by an organization calling itself "Save Fenway Park (SFP)!" Members acted in a spirit nicely articulated by "ballpark advocate" Michael Betzold of Detroit: "Battling to preserve a special place is not quaint provincialism. It is defiance against the relentless obliteration of memory and community."

The Red Sox owners backed down, and in 2002 they sold the team to John Henry, Tom Werner, and Larry Lucchino. Club president and CEO Lucchino has assured Red Sox fans that the team "will remain at Fenway Park for the long term. There is a kind of magic in the place—an energy and a history that is impossible to duplicate."

Quite right he is. Fenway Park is about a present filled with the past, filled with shared memories of losing after coming so close, of the young Babe Ruth, of Ted Williams and Carlton Fisk and Carl Yastrzemski and Curt Schilling, of contests against the hated Yankees—of an earlier and better America. Such memories help to form and to maintain communities. But not only does Fenway Park trigger shared memories; it stands for continuity in a country not nearly as much in love with "change" as it sometimes imagines itself to be. It is a standing rebuke to those modern parks which are utterly a-historical and more about entertainment, commercialism, comforts, and fashionable foods than about baseball and tradition. For Red Sox fans, in contrast, Fenway is "like my second home," as one of them told sociologist Michael Ian Borer.

Fenway Park and Wrigley Field are the parks that true

baseball fans, even those who live outside of Boston and Chicago, long to see before they die. Those old enough and lucky enough to have been to games played in some of the old parks that did not survive cherish their memories. I still remember the horseshoe-shaped Polo Grounds, home of the New York Giants from 1911 to 1957. Talk about quirks and bizarre dimensions! Squeezed into the land available, it measured 279 feet down the line in left and a mere 257 down the line in right; whether a player swung from the right or left side, if he pulled the ball he could hit a home run with little more than a pop up—an art perfected by Dusty Rhodes. But if the ball was hit toward dead center it had to travel some 475 feet to clear the fence.

The Polo Grounds was the site of some of baseball's greatest moments, Willie Mays's "catch" and Bobby Thomson's "shot heard round the world" among them. Many Giant fans never forgave owner Horace Stoneham for moving the team out of the historic field—and out of New York. On the lookout for greater profits and impressed by the Braves' move from Boston to Milwaukee, Stoneham let Dodger owner Walter O'Malley talk him into a move to California. The Dodgers' move meant the death of Brooklyn's Ebbets Field—"the shrine," according to Roger Kahn—as well. It is true that both the Polo Grounds and Ebbets Field were in poor condition and that the Flatbush neighborhood in Brooklyn had become less safe, but with the eventual destruction of the old parks—the New York Mets played in the Polo Grounds in 1962 and 1963—a part of baseball died.

An even greater part died when, at the close of the 2008 season, the Yankees abandoned Yankee Stadium for a new "Yankee Stadium." Opened in the Bronx at the beginning of the 1923 season, the old stadium was known from the first as the "House That Ruth Built." In the over eight decades of its existence, Yankee Stadium was the venue for thirty-seven World Series and four All-Star games. More than two dozen Hall of Famers called it home. Ruth, Gehrig, DiMaggio, Mantle, Berra—the list is long and awe-inspiring. The stadium had undergone needed renovation during the 1974 and 1975 seasons (the team played home games in those years at the Mets' Shea Stadium—which has given way to the new Citi Field). As a result, there was some serious loss, but at least its concrete-and-steel bones remained.

The new Yankee Stadium, across East 161st street, is a hugely expensive effort to mimic some of the original while increasing the amenities. Monument Park—consisting of statues and plaques that commemorate Yankee greats of the past—migrated over, and a "Great Hall," another tribute to the team's history, has been added. Still, the place seems less concerned with baseball than with luxury suites and shi-shi food and drink. Hot dogs and beer are apparently too plebeian for the high rollers who almost alone can afford the price of admission. Yankee Stadium II has an upscale steakhouse, a martini bar, and the Mohegan Sun Sports Bar, which offers two full bars and truffle fries. None of this is likely to change the mind of the Yankee fan interviewed by the *New York Times* during the last game played in Yankee Stadium I. "The new Yankee Stadium will never be like this one," he said. "It's kind of like when you fall in love. You fall in love once, and you fall in love with one stadium."

Yankee Stadium II is among the so-called "retro" ball parks, the first of which was Baltimore's Camden Yards, opened in 1992. I have attended games there and at Coors Field (Denver) and Nationals Park (Washington, D.C.). They are a great improvement over the infamous multipurpose "superstadiums" of the '60s, '70s, and '80s, most of which were designed primarily for football. These "cookie-cutter" parks were characterized by symmetrical fields, artificial turf, and huge seating capacities. Some, like the Houston Astrodome (1965–99), were enclosed. Almost always, they were surrounded by gigantic parking lots. Lacking individuality, and hence charm, they all looked alike.

Camden Yards changed things; since 1992, virtually every new park has been retro in design. Insofar as they mimic the classic parks like Wrigley and Fenway, they are to be praised. And yet they are not classic parks; they are consciously *planned* imitations. So while they witness, by their designs, to a longing for the past, they cannot recreate authenticity. Inevitably, they all look rather like Camden Yards! Still, they are probably the best we can hope for; they at least pay homage to the importance of memory and of place. Writing in the *New York Times* in 1994, Paul Goldberger had this to say: "Baseball is connected intimately to the place in which it is played and derives much of its aura from that place."

Another of the unhappy results of all this movement—to new ballparks, new cities, and new teams—is that teams can rise (or fall) in the standings in ways that further destroy continuity. "Until 1990 there had been no 'worst-to-first' volatility in [the twentieth] century—no team won a pennant the year after finishing last. The Twins and Braves did in 1991 and the Phillies did in 1993. The 1993 A's were the first team since 1915—the A's Philadelphia ancestors—to finish alone in last place the year after finishing first." George Will wrote this as though it is cause for celebration. But is it? What he describes is a situation that does not reward the orderly and thoughtful building of a long-term winner, but rather a quick fix, a crap shoot, chaos. It should be deplored, not celebrated.

In addition to its admirable continuities, fifties baseball was a game first and a business second. It is no accident, as Marxists like to say, that a book about the 1950s Dodgers was titled *The Boys of Summer*, while Will titled his book about the modern game *Men at Work*. "When I played," Andy Pafko has said with some exaggeration, "it was strictly a sport." But he was certainly right that "now, it's big business, plain and simple. It's still a great game, it's baseball, but the game has changed." It seemed to Brady Greer "that greed—greedy owners and greedy players—was a virus ever more virulent, coursing through the sport's veins."

One of the surest signs that baseball had become a business first and a sport a distant second was the growing power of the Major League Baseball Players Association. Formed in 1953, the union possessed little influence until it hired Marvin Miller as its executive director in 1966. An experienced labor economist and a skilled union negotiator, Miller had both a principled and a visceral dislike of team owners, and he turned the Players Association into one of the nation's most powerful unions. He helped make it possible for players to become very rich men. Like all union leaders, of course, he used the strike, or the threat of a strike, as the means to get what he wanted.

On April 1, 1972, the Miller-led players walked out, but they returned 13 days later when owners agreed to a process of salary arbitration. The missed games were never made up and as one unintended result the Tigers played one more game than the Red Sox and won the American League East Division by a half game; it was a sign of the times that business had trumped the game's integrity. On June 12, 1981, the players went on strike again, this time because owners were demanding compensation, in the form of an unprotected player from the signing team's roster, for any loss of a free agent. The strike ended with a compromise settlement on July 31. Teams that lost a star player could be compensated with an unprotected player from any team, and the players agreed to limit free agency to those who had had at least six years in the Show. Because 713 games had been cancelled, baseball adopted a complicated and unsatisfactory "split season" playoff schedule.

In 1985, Donald Fehr, who has described himself as an unrepentant sixties radical, became executive director of the Players Association. He was almost immediately confronted with a clear case of owner collusion: from 1985 to 1987, the owners declined to bid for the services of free agents. In the end, arbitrators fined them for violating the 1968 Collective Bargaining Agreement. Fehr neither forgave nor forgot, and in 1994 he orchestrated a strike, primarily over the owners' effort to impose a cap on salaries.

This was the most devastating strike in the game's history. On August 12, the players walked out, and on September 14, no progress in the negotiations having been made, Acting Commissioner Bud Selig (an owner of the Milwaukee Brewers) called off the rest of the season, including the World Series. The strike came to an end on April 2, 1995, but only after federal judge Sonia Sotomayor, now an Associate Justice of the Supreme Court, issued a preliminary injunction against the owners. The fictional Brady Greer was not alone in wishing a pox on both the owners and the players' houses. Fans across the nation were incensed because wealthy owners and wealthy players had placed their business interests above their devotion to and respect for the *game*.

But fan anger, though real enough, was short-lived. Baseball dreamed up a number of gimmicks designed to spark interest and lure all but the most indignant back to the ballpark. In 1995, two wild-card teams—those boasting the best record among the leagues' non-divisional winners—were awarded spots in the playoffs. From then on, a second-place divisional finisher could win the World Series! Two years later, Commissioner Selig instituted regular-season interleague play. No doubt New York fans were excited by the prospect of Yankee-Met games, but were Blue Jay fans looking forward to seeing the Florida Marlins? This "innovation" has had the effect of destroying the mystique that once surrounded the World Series. In baseball—as in life—the burden of proof should always rest on those who advocate change, not on those who stand for continuity.

In 1995, fortune smiled on the game when Cal Ripken, Jr., the Baltimore Orioles' standout, broke Lou Gehrig's consecutive game record of 2,130—a streak that had once seemed unsurpassable. Just as important, as subsequent events would prove, Ripken was scandal free, a role model for fans of all ages. And yet baseball officials, owners, and players were becoming increasingly aware that the game was no longer the national pastime. Young people in particular found baseball to be too slow moving, too boring; they preferred football and basketball, not to mention movies and rock concerts. For them baseball was just another form of entertainment, and not a very exciting one at that. What then could baseball do to compete successfully? Emphasize pitching and defense? No, the answer seemed to be to encourage offense, especially in the form of the home run.

It was to that end that the American League, in 1973, had

introduced the "Designated Hitter" (DH), who would bat in place of the pitcher. For traditionalist fans, the DH was, and remains, an obscenity, not least because it removes some of the game's most important strategic decisions. Should the manager leave in his pitcher, who may be doing well, or should he remove him for a pinch hitter in an effort to get a needed run late in the game?

The DH rule did produce more offense, but the National League wisely refused to adopt it and, in any event, taking the bat out of the hands of weak-hitting pitchers was not enough to win over young fans. New ways would have to be found to produce more power hitting. A decision was made to narrow the strike zone and to prohibit pitchers from brushing hitters back, thus reducing the important element of fear at the plate. When people think of "knockdown" pitches, they tend to think of beanballs, pitches aimed at a batter's head. But as anyone who has played the game knows, a pitch at the head is relatively easy to duck. A problem arises only if, like Ray Chapman, a batter freezes. If a pitcher intends to hit you in the head, he will throw the ball behind you, shoulder high. Instinct makes you duck backward—into the path of the ball.

A pitcher may attempt to hit a batter, but he usually aims at the ribs or thighs. At major league speeds, it will hurt, but it is not designed to do permanent damage. Inside, especially high inside, pitches are a pitcher's way of keeping a batter from digging in at the plate. It plants uncertainty in his mind and throws his timing off. To disallow knockdown pitches is to give hitters, especially major league hitters, a decided advantage. Some pitchers—one thinks of Sal "The Barber" Maglie, Early Wynn, Don Drysdale— are famous/infamous for knocking hitters down. Some, like Christy Mathewson or Carl Erskine, never threw at hitters. But most pitchers have regarded knockdown pitches as legitimate weapons in their eternal war against hitters.

And so have the hitters themselves. "See, in those days [the 1950s], we had knockdowns," Eddie Mathews testified. "If a batter was having a lot of success against a pitcher or against his team, the pitcher would knock him down. He wouldn't necessarily hit you, but he would throw inside or near your head. We pretty much accepted that fact." Not any more. Up-and-in pitches regularly produce glares from hitters, many of whom are ready to charge the mound if they are decked. With umpires ready to eject a pitcher for throwing high and tight, hitters gain a distinct edge.

That was the whole point as far as the Major Leagues were concerned. The effort to produce more home runs proved remarkably successful. In the 1990s, even players who had never been known as power hitters began to belt homers with eye-popping frequency. Consider the case of Baltimore center fielder and lead-off man Brady Anderson. In 1993, 1994, and 1995, Anderson hit a combined total of 41 round-trippers; in 1996, he hammered 50. Jose Canseco, one of the game's greatest sluggers, thought he knew why. "Was he using steroids? I never saw him inject himself, but he and I discussed steroids many times. And consider this: How else could someone go from hitting a total of forty-one home runs over three seasons to cranking out fifty in one, without a major boost from steroids?"

Canseco's opinion carried weight because, as we now know, he was the "Godfather of Steroids," the player who, more than any other, led baseball into a scandalous "steroid era." Athletes use anabolic steroids primarily to build muscles. But Canseco, who began to inject himself in 1985, testified that they also improve hand-eye coordination and increase recuperative powers. Although they have been outlawed in the United States since 1990, baseball players continued to use steroids for the simple reason that they enhance performance—particularly with respect to the power game—and in that way make possible higher salaries. "If," Canseco wrote in his unapologetic book *Juiced*, "you get bigger, stronger, and can hit more home runs, you can make a lot more money." Highpockets did not know how right he was.

The owners, too, wanted more home runs, and in 1998 Mark McGwire of the Cardinals and Sammy Sosa of the Cubs obliged them. Like Mantle and Maris in 1961, the two sluggers chased the season record for most home runs—but unlike the Yankee greats, they were helped along by steroids. McGwire has finally admitted as much. In 2005, when the House Government Reform Committee subpoenaed him, he refused to answer questions concerning his possible use. His mantra was: "I'm not here to talk about the past." And he continued to deny that Canseco injected him. The latter's testimony was, however, compelling. "Steroids made Mark much bigger and much stronger; perhaps most important of all, I personally observed how they made him feel more confident and more comfortable with his own body. All of that definitely helped him break Roger Maris's record in 1998."

McGwire did not merely break Maris's record—he shattered it by hitting an astounding 70 home runs. Just as incredible, Sosa, with 66, was not far behind. Canseco did not know the Cub outfielder, but he pointed out, rightly, that Sosa had bulked up rather suddenly. In his first nine seasons in the major leagues, he hit as many as 40 home runs only once. After hitting 66 in 1998, he hit 63 in 1999, 50 in 2000, and 64 in 2001. This is more than a little suspicious. Sosa admitted using creatine, a legal muscle builder, but before the House committee he denied using steroids—sort of. He seemed suddenly to have difficulty understanding English. In June 2009, the *New York Times* reported that he was among those players who tested positive for performance-enhancing drugs (PEDs) in 2003.

Sosa and McGwire were not the only players putting up unprecedented home run numbers. From 1876 to 1994, the 50-home run mark was reached only eighteen times; Hank Aaron, Frank Robinson, Reggie Jackson, Mike Schmidt, Ted Williams, Ernie Banks, and Eddie Mathews all failed to reach it. But from 1995 to 2002, the 50 mark was reached another eighteen times, often by hitters who had never previously demonstrated much power. Of Brady Anderson we have already spoken. Luis Gonzalez never hit more than 26 home runs in a season. In 2000, he hit 31. In 2001, he went on a rampage, belting 57!

Gonzalez and Anderson were relatively small fry, and so, except for one MVP year, was the late Ken Caminiti. A cocaine user, Caminiti confessed to *Sports Illustrated* that his monster season was a result of using steroids. Other juicers, however, were among the game's elite. In testimony before a grand jury, Jason Giambi confessed to using steroids and human growth hormone (another anabolic). Canseco fingered the sweet-swinging Rafael Palmeiro, who, under oath, denied ever using steroids ("I have never used steroids, period"), only to test positive for stanozolol, a potent steroid. Gary Sheffield denied ever *knowingly* using steroids, though there is considerable evidence that he was being less than truthful.

And then there is Barry Bonds, who now holds the single-season (73) and career (762) records for most home runs. Bonds, too, has denied ever knowingly using steroids, but evidence to the contrary, set out in detail in Mark Fainaru-Wada and Lance Williams's *Game of Shadows*, is all but irrefutable. "Of the five best offensive seasons in Bonds's career," the investigative reporters pointed out, "four came after he was 35 years old—and after 1999, the year he began using steroids." But Bonds is not the only superstar to perform unusual feats at a relatively advanced baseball age. At 36 and 37 (1999; 2000), Roger Clemens, "The Rocket," had, for him, modest years with the Yankees: he went 14-10 and 13-8. But at 38, he won 20 and lost only 3 and at 41 he was 18-4. He seemed to have discovered the fountain of youth.

Thrilled to watch Clemens pitch, fans set aside any suspicions they may have had—until his personal trainer, Brian McNamee, testified under oath that he had injected the once certain Hall of Famer with steroids. Clemens denied the charge, under oath. Obviously, one of them lied and Clemens had more reason to do so. He continues to protest his innocence, but the number of those willing to believe him grows ever smaller.

Not every superstar is, as they say, in denial. The gifted Alex Rodriguez has admitted that he used steroids during the three years he played for the Texas Rangers. He described himself as young and naïve, but he was 25-27 at the time. What is not in doubt is that he put up impressive numbers: In 2001 he hit 52 home runs; in 2002, 57; in 2003, 47. But many in the press and in the stands continue to discuss his chances of overtaking Bonds—

as though his cheating for at least three years is of no consequence now that he has confessed (after being outed by *Sports Illustrated*).

Playing for the Indians, Red Sox, and Dodgers, Manny Ramirez has also established himself as one of the greatest sluggers in baseball history. He has over 500 career home runs. In 2008, at age 36, his slugging percentage was .601. Only five other players that old had ever had a higher percentage: Bonds (whom we won't count), Babe Ruth, Ted Williams, Stan Musial, and Hank Aaron. Word, however, has leaked out that Ramirez tested positive for PEDs in 2003. This, after March 2009 drug tests showed an elevated level of testosterone in his system. The slugging outfielder's agent, Scott Boras, explained that his charge was under a doctor's care for a "personal health issue." Major League officials then asked for and received Ramirez's medical files. They revealed that he had been prescribed human chorionic gonadotropin (hCG), a female fertility drug sometimes given to men with a reproductive-system defect that results in low sperm development, but also taken by steroid users to restart their body's natural testosterone production as they come off a steroid cycle. The league suspended Ramirez for 50 games.

Not long enough, if the league had listened to David Ortiz, Ramirez's power-hitting teammate when he played for the Red Sox. Ortiz had once sternly suggested mandatory one-year suspensions for drug violations. Of course, that was before the *New York Times* reported that he too was on the list of players who tested positive for PEDs in 2003. Ortiz's defense was that he was careless in his use of supplements and vitamins. Baseball, including the commissioner's office, claimed to believe him. His career record, however, is suspicious. As a member of the Minnesota Twins from 1997 to 2002, he never hit more than 20 home runs. In 2003, his first year with the Red Sox, he socked 31. He then went on a spree: 41 homers in 2004; 47 in 2005; 54 in 2006; 35 in 2007. Because he and Ramirez contributed so much to the Red Sox's World Championships in 2004 and 2007, one is entitled to ask whether or not the curse of the Bambino has really been broken.

In fact, the steroid scandal raises the whole issue of baseball records, sacred in a way that football and basketball's are not. Nothing much can be done about team achievements, those due in part to cheating players—though asterisks should be considered. But what about the individual cheaters? Retired Senator Jim Bunning of Kentucky, a Hall of Fame pitcher, believes that all individual records tainted by steroids should be wiped out—and he is right. At the very least, steroid users should be barred from the Hall of Fame.

It is telling that one of the recurrent themes (and rationalizations) in the testimonies of players who used steroids, or were accused of having used steroids, is that baseball is no longer a game—it is merely a form of entertainment. Here is Jose Canseco: "I always saw myself as more of an entertainer than a baseball player, and I was always very up front about it." Jason Giambi: "Why do fans always complain about how much money we make? I mean, nobody complains that Tom Hanks makes $20 million per picture. That's all we are. We're in the entertainment business." Barry Bonds: "We're entertainers. Let us entertain."

There is much to this. Baseball since the fifties has steadily lost its ability to elevate our sense of human possibility. The players are no longer heroes who inspire; they are mortals who entertain, mercenaries whose loyalty to team and city is contingent upon the success or failure of their agent's most recent negotiations with management. They have become, in short, our baser rather than our nobler selves.

Remembering baseball in the fifties evokes other memories of the decade. David Halberstam makes much, for example, of Elvis Presley. "A new generation of Americans was breaking away from the habits of its parents and defining itself by its music," he reported. Unfortunately, it was what Milan Kundera has called "music minus memory, the music in which the bones of Beethoven and Ellington, the dust of Palestrina and Schönberg, lie buried." The Czech writer mentioned Duke Ellington because he wished to include popular music, one of America's gifts to the world, in his list of what has been lost. As Joseph Epstein has written, American popular music of the late 1940s and early 1950s "was not of interest only to the young." Many forget that Elvis burst on the scene in the *second half* of the decade—for someone like me, born in 1939, the fifties did not mean "you ain't nothin' but a hound dog." (One would not, of course, wish to make extravagant claims for some of what I and my generation listened to in the fifties—"Sh-Boom" by the Crew-Cuts won't make anyone's list of standards.)

Still, if popular tunes were not exactly sophisticated, neither were they morally repugnant. And the singers did more than scream and gyrate. I am not alone in remembering groups like the Four Aces, the Four Lads, and the Ames Brothers; male vocalists (as they were then called) such as Vic Damone, the elegant Nat King Cole, the still more elegant Billy Eckstine, and the über-relaxed Dean Martin; and female vocalists like June Christy, Kay Starr, Patti Page, and Julie London. At a more sophisticated level, some of the greatest of the popular artists were still around: Louis Armstrong, Ella Fitzgerald, Fred Astaire, Tony Bennett, Judy Garland, Peggy Lee, Mel Tormé, Bing Crosby—and Roger Maris's favorite, Frank Sinatra.

Ol' Blue Eyes was in Leo Durocher's box the day that Thomson hit "the shot heard round the world." His divorce from Nancy Barbato would soon be final and, on November 7, 1951, he married Ava Gardner, with whom he had been involved since 1949. Their marriage proved to be as stormy as their affair, and the couple separated in 1953. The LPs (long-playing records), introduced in 1948, were just then coming into their own against the older 78- and 45-rpm singles, and Sinatra recognized that they represented the future (in fact, they are presently making something of a comeback). In 1955, Capitol released one of the finest LPs ever recorded—"Frank Sinatra: In the Wee Small Hours." Unlike earlier song collections, this one revolved around a single concept—the pain of a lost love.

Blessed with Nelson Riddle's arrangements and inspired—if that is the word—by Sinatra's breakup with Gardner, the album, with the title song and such classics as "Mood Indigo," "I Get Along Without You Very Well," and "When Your Lover Has Gone," established and maintained a mood of melancholy that was as authentic as it was moving. As critic John Rockwell has written, "Ava Gardner may have left scars, but as happens so often with great artists, personal pain translated into artistic achievement." Sinatra's career was far from over, but it was in the 1950s that he was at his very best.

Sinatra and the other great singers of his time—Crosby, Astaire, Bennett, Tormé—were fortunate that they lived at a time when America was home to the most gifted songwriters in the world: Irving Berlin, George and Ira Gershwin, Jerome Kern, Cole Porter, Johnny Mercer, Richard Rodgers and Lawrence Hart and Oscar Hammerstein, Hoagy Carmichael, Jimmy Van Heusen, Jule Styne, Sammy Cahn, Duke Ellington. These men composed the "standards," songs that will last as long, but no longer, as civilization itself. Most of them were written between 1925 and 1950 and were known to all musically literate Americans, young and old, in the 1950s—that is PR, or pre-rock.

It was in the fifties, too, that the golden age of the musical theater neared its end. We are not likely to see again shows such as Adler and Ross's *Damn Yankees*, Jerome Kern's *Showboat*, Cole Porter's *Kiss Me, Kate*, Alan Jay Lerner and Frederick Loewe's *My Fair Lady*, Richard Rodgers and Oscar Hammerstein's *Carousel* and *South Pacific*, or George Gershwin's *Porgy and Bess* (a musical or an opera?). As Wilfrid Sheed observed, the music and lyrics these men wrote constitute "far and away our greatest contribution to the world's art supply in the so-called American Century."

The fifties also marked the end of the golden age of radio—and of American comedy. On Sunday evening, millions of Americans gathered around the radio to listen to "The Jack Benny Show." Born Benjamin Kubelsky in Chicago and raised in Waukegan, Benny showed youthful promise as a baseball player. He once played on a semi-pro team with Bob O'Farrell, who later put in 21 seasons with four National League teams and won the

1926 Most Valuable Player award as a member of the St. Louis Cardinals. Benny was an avid fan—Hollywood Stars and Los Angeles Dodgers—throughout his life, and often talked baseball with Leo Durocher. But he was destined to be a comedian, one of the most memorable we have ever had. "I realized," he wrote in a posthumously published autobiography, "I was part of the memories of growing up in America."

So he was. Was there a single American, in the 1940s and 1950s, who did not know that "Jack"—the radio character Jack—was "39"? Or that he was a notorious skinflint (in reality, he was a generous man)? There were endless jokes about his stinginess, but what might be called "The Joke" went like this: Jack is walking home at night when a holdup man shoves a gun in his ribs. "Your money or your life," he snarls. There is an extended pause—Benny was the master of the pause, of *timing*. "Come on, hurry up," the holdup man commands. To which Jack finally replies: "*I'm thinking it over.*"

The radio audience heard sound effects of Jack's footsteps, and then those of the holdup man. Benny was able to exploit all of radio's possibilities, its ability to stimulate the imagination. As he put it, he and other radio comedians such as Fred Allen, Eddie Cantor, and Edgar Bergen "learned how to orchestrate voices, sound effects, pauses, silences, shrill voices, growls, eerie voices—and we strived to build moments and scenes just for the *ear*. We found out that if you have the ear, the outline and the colors, a picture was painted in the mind's eye. It was fabulous what the human imagination was able to project to itself." Precisely why baseball, too, was better on radio.

Benny also recognized the importance of a supporting cast, and he had one of the best in the business: his real-life wife Mary Livingstone, Phil Harris, Dennis Day, Don Wilson, and, above all, the inimitable Eddie Anderson, "Rochester van Jones." Black, and with a permanent case of laryngitis, Anderson began his career in vaudeville and played "Noah" in the movie version of *The Green Pastures* (1936). He was a comedian of rare talent whom Benny hired not because he sought to promote civil rights but because Anderson was so good. Together they made radio history.

Benny sometimes received angry letters because his radio character paid Rochester so little money. One communication so incensed him that he decided to reply. "For your information," he wrote, "'Rochester' lives in a ten-room house, he has two servants serving him, he has three cars, a stable of horses and is now in the market for a cabin cruiser." He was then making $150,000 a year. But there was something more, something more important. Benny put it this way: "Even in the [early] days when he played the most negative stereotyped minstrel character, Rochester was never a servile, supplicating Stepin Fetchit. I was as much the fall guy for Rochester as I was for Phil Harris or Mary Livingstone." That is true, and there is no doubt that Rochester played a small but real role in changing the country's mind about racial discrimination.

Jack's radio show continued on the air until 1955, but, recognizing the importance of a new medium, he began a television show in 1950. He was able to stay on until 1965, an amazing run, thanks to his hitherto unused talents as a visual comedian—he could get laughs simply by turning his head toward the audience and giving them that *look*. And yet he was never really at home on TV. "In radio," he observed in his autobiography, "people loved me in a different way. I came at them gently—quietly, through their ears. I suggested subtle images to them, picture jokes. I was like a friendly uncle, a slightly eccentric mad uncle—now I became something else, too much. The television camera is like a magnifying glass and you can't enjoy looking at anything so blown up for too long."

Benny was right when he observed that "to survive even five years with a regular weekly [television] program is damn near impossible." *Your Show of Shows*, which featured the gifted Sid Caesar and the wonderfully zany Imogene Coca, lasted four seasons (1950–1954); George Gobel made it for six (1954–1960). Not even Bob Newhart could do much better in the seventies and eighties; *The Bob Newhart Show* was on for six seasons (1972–1978)

108

and *Newhart* for nine (1981–1990). But despite his undeniable talent for sit-coms, Newhart was at his best as a standup comedian, one who used pauses and a natural stammer to almost perfect effect. He burst on the scene at the end of the fifties with a now classic album: *The Button-Down Mind of Bob Newhart* (1960).

"The greatest comedian I've ever seen," Newhart wrote in *I Shouldn't Even Be Doing This! And Other Things That Strike Me as Funny*, "is Jack Benny." He himself is arguably the greatest comedian of a later generation. Like Benny, he came from the Chicago suburbs—Oak Park and Austin in his case—and stayed clear of political subjects. Nor did he stoop to locker-room humor. And like Benny, he has a perfect sense of timing. His standup bits are classics of their kind. Many of us all but memorized some of them—the "Driving Instructor" for example. Or "Nobody Will Ever Play Baseball." Newhart is a Cub fan who can still name, from memory, the starting lineup of the 1945 pennant-winning team. But in his imaginary conversation with Abner Doubleday, he makes the game sound utterly ridiculous.

Newhart speaks with pride of the statue of him, as the television character Dr. Bob Hartley, at the entrance to Chicago's Navy Pier—rather, he says, like the statue of Jackie Gleason, as bus driver Ralph Kramden, which stands at the entrance to the Port Authority Bus Terminal in New York. Unlike Benny and Newhart, who were verbal comedians, Gleason was a visual comedian, a man born for television. In different show formats, "The Great One" created unforgettable characters in the knowledge that he could not survive week after week only as himself. There was Reggie Van Gleason III, a boozy playboy; Joe the Bartender, a homespun philosopher; Fenwick Babbitt, an innocent who was always given impossible work, usually having to do with a conveyer belt that moved faster and faster; and the Poor Soul, a silent character who reminded one of a heavier Charlie Chaplin.

The first *Honeymooner* skit aired two days—that is, October 5, 1951—after Gleason attended the game in which Thomson hit his famous home run. Gleason played Kramden, a man frustrated by his humble employment and salary and out to prove to himself and others that he was really a big shot. His wife Alice, played first by Pert Kelton and then by Audrey Meadows, was always deflating his balloon, thus throwing Ralph into a rage ("you're going to the moon, Alice" or "one of these days, Alice, pow! right in the kisser"), which left her, and an audience that knew he had a good heart, unmoved.

Ralph tried repeatedly to enlist neighbor Ed Norton (played by Art Carney), a sewer worker, in some scheme to strike it rich— and in that way to satisfy his ego and, more important, impress Alice. When, inevitably, his plans failed, Alice was always there to forgive and love him. Most episodes ended with a sheepish and grateful Ralph saying to her "baby, you're the greatest" and giving her a big kiss.

The Honeymooners was so popular that Gleason decided to turn it into an independent show. It debuted as a half-hour comedy in 1955, but because of falling ratings it lasted only a year. When, however, re-runs began, the show was recognized for what it was—a television classic.

In *The Fifties*, David Halberstam devoted an entire chapter to the "Beat" writers—Jack Kerouac, Allen Ginsberg, Gregory Corso. But while they may be of some interest to those with a taste for social history, they were, and are, of little interest to students of serious literature. Not, certainly, in a decade in which novelists like Ernest Hemingway, William Faulkner, Saul Bellow, and Ralph Ellison, and poets such as T. S. Eliot, Robert Frost, Wallace Stevens, and W. H. Auden, were still at work. Not when Flannery O'Connor, perhaps the finest American writer of the postwar era, was writing some of her shattering stories. And along with O'-Connor, of course, distinguished Southern writers such as John Crowe Ransom, Allen Tate, Robert Penn Warren, Andrew Nelson Lytle, and Donald Davidson were still active.

Unlike the 1960s, it was a serious decade. One could pick up a copy of *Partisan Review* and find work by Vladimir Nabokov, Isaac Bashevis Singer, Jacques Barzun, Lionel Trilling, Dwight

Macdonald, George Orwell, and T. S. Eliot. Always leftist—though staunchly anti-Stalinist—in outlook, the *Review* maintained high literary standards. The same may be said of *Encounter*, published in England with covert funding from the CIA. In its pages, one could read work by Robert Graves, Isaiah Berlin, Edmund Wilson, James Agee, Arthur Koestler, Michael Polanyi, George Kennan, and many other important thinkers and writers.

The general editorial outlook of *Encounter* was social-democratic, though its fierce opposition to communism was in keeping with the conservative intellectual climate of the 1950s, in America as well as in Europe. Two Americans, Louis Fischer and Richard Wright, contributed to the 1949 volume *The God That Failed*, which chronicled the disillusion with communism experienced by six intellectuals, no one of whom could be described as a conservative. The case of James Burnham is more difficult to judge. A professor of philosophy at New York University and a onetime Trotskyite, Burnham lost his radical faith and became an influential voice on the American right. This had everything to do with his fervent anticommunism, which sometimes led him to advocate reckless policies when dealing with the Soviet Union.

The Soviet suppression of the 1956 Hungarian Revolution gave increased weight to the opinions of Burnham and other anticommunist writers, many of whom were of "the god that failed" school. Whittaker Chambers was one of the most impressive. It was he who identified Alger Hiss as a Soviet agent—a truth of which there is no longer any reasonable doubt—and it was he who wrote the powerful and moving *Witness* (1952). When all is said and done, he knew from experience that communism, unlike anticommunism, proclaimed a faith; and faith he wrote in a Dostoevskian vein, "is the central problem of this age. The Western world does not know it, but it already possesses the answer to this problem—but only provided that its faith in God and the freedom He enjoins is as great as communism's faith in Man."

At the time that Chambers's book appeared, faith in the Christian God, and with it confidence in Judeo-Christian morality, was still very much alive in most Americans. Christian faith was not considered to be strictly a private matter; it played a pivotal role in communal life, especially as a foundation for morality. Not even unbelievers conspired to drive Christianity out of the public square. Everyone knew of, and most admired, Billy Graham, the charismatic evangelist and spiritual adviser to presidents. It was not only Catholics who watched Bishop Fulton J. Sheen on the television show *Life is Worth Living*.

T. S. Eliot's *Four Quartets* and Reinhold Niebuhr's *The Nature and Destiny of Man* explored faith and freedom on a more sophisticated level—too sophisticated for some readers. More popular in America, but every bit as serious as Eliot and Niebuhr, was C.S. Lewis, the Oxford don and author of numerous books of Christian apologetics, including *Mere Christianity* and *The Screwtape Letters*, as well as the seven-volume *Chronicles of Narnia*, a Christian fantasy for children. In the 1950s, Lewis's Oxford colleague and friend J. R. R. Tolkien gave the English-speaking world the three-volume romance *Lord of the Rings*, in which Christian themes predominate. Although the romance was enjoyed by the young, Tolkien wrote for adults.

Christianity and the Judeo-Christian moral tradition that the vast majority of Americans took to be authoritative (whether or not they obeyed all of its commands) lent to the fifties a stability, a respect for authority, and a sense of community that have been lost. In fact, a feeling of loss is usually central to those of us old enough to remember the fifties. One of the most obvious losses is the freedom to stroll city streets at night without fear; another is the freedom to allow children to play outside without watchful supervision. In a 1995 program about Chicago in the 1940s and 1950s telecast by the city's public channel, aging Chicagoans, black and white, recalled the joys of being outdoors, even sleeping in the front yard during heat waves, without fear of crime.

Schools too were safe; one did not expect to pick up the morning newspaper to find that someone had gunned down students at an elementary school, a high school, or a university. Schools were not places where drugs circulated or young people had sex. They were places of learning where teachers and administrators maintained a necessary and proper discipline and did not question the legitimacy of their own authority. Parents backed them up; they did not phone their attorney and threaten to sue the school when their child was disciplined or received a poor grade. Those in authority did not take the later view that all students were equal in intelligence, that they had a "right" to do anything they wished, or that there was no "good" or "bad" but only "different" behavior.

In the 1950s, common people (as opposed to intellectuals) did not believe that ill behavior could be explained, or explained away, by something outside the perpetrator, something over which he had no control. They did not turn to armies of sociologists and psychologists for enlightenment concerning the "deeper" causes of crime. They believed in character, in personal responsibility. As Alan Ehrenhalt wrote in *Lost City: The Forgotten Virtues of Community in America*: "In Chicago in the 1950s, there were no complex societal explanations of bad behavior, no histories of child abuse or substance abuse or low self-esteem, no failure on the part of insensitive parents or authorities. The explanation was that these were bad people—sinners."

The notion of sin was deeply embedded in a society that had not yet cut itself loose from its Judeo-Christian heritage. It has been replaced by saying that an action impossible to defend is "inappropriate," as though one were speaking of using the wrong fork at a formal dinner; or by elevating "racism" or "sexism" to the level of original sins, so strong in their hold on those accused that they may not even be fully conscious of them. This peculiar attitude is evidence of the longing for religion, for a belief in something beyond one's self, something that gives meaning and direction to a life.

One of the greatest losses since the fifties is that of the traditional family. Partisans of the sixties, few of whom were alive and aware in the fifties, never tire of telling us that the kind of family portrayed on the television program *Ozzie and Harriet* never existed. The Nelsons were happily married, with two boys. To be sure, *Ozzie and Harriet* was a television show and, unlike later shows, husband and wife did not scream at each other or have to endure the insolence of their boys. The family was idealized (Ozzie, for example, never seemed to work), but it was not in fact very different from many real-life families in the fifties.

No one doubts that behind closed doors families in the fifties had their problems and difficulties, cruelties and hurts. But couples did not divorce because one or both of them got a better offer, or because they wanted to make another "choice," or because they wished to find themselves, or because their needs were not being met. "Growing up in the 50s," Joseph Epstein has written, he "had no friends whose parents had played the rough trick on them of divorcing." I had only two classmates whose parents divorced.

People stayed together because they did not believe that being free to choose was the only, much less the most important, value. They felt a responsibility to their children and to their spouse, however alienated they might be. They did not believe that they lived in a world of limitless options; maturity, they knew, depended upon a recognition and acceptance of limits. Sometimes staying together meant unhappiness, but they were aware, however sadly, that there are considerations other than personal happiness, including considerations of responsibility to oneself and others. They did not know, but probably guessed, that those who divorced did not always find the happiness they so desperately sought.

One of the charges routinely leveled against America in the fifties is that the country discriminated against its black citizens. Of this there is no doubt. We have seen that although the color line had been broken in baseball, black players still could not stay in the same hotel as their white teammates. In Chicago, blacks lived almost exclusively on the south and west sides—those of us who lived in the suburbs rarely encountered a black person, unless he or she came out of the city to do yard work or clean house.

During the years I attended Oak Park and River Forest (IL) High School—1953–1957—only one student was black; he was Percy Julian Jr. His father, Dr. Percy Julian, was a distinguished chemist who had moved his family to Oak Park late in 1950. On June 12, 1951, someone tried to dynamite the Julian residence.

Things then were not as they should have been, but they were beginning to change, and in significant ways. Many in Oak Park rallied to Dr. Julian and his family's side. The conscience of Americans was beginning to awaken; public opinion polls in the 1950s registered a spectacular change in white attitudes toward blacks. By 1959, 56 percent of whites favored the integration of schools. In understated ways, ballplayers like Ernie Banks, Henry Aaron, and Willie Mays—and beloved performers such as Louis Armstrong, Ella Fitzgerald, Lena Horne, and Eddie "Rochester" Anderson—helped to produce a change of hearts. It is important to remember that it was in 1954—not the sixties—that the U.S. Supreme Court held in *Brown v. Board of Education of Topeka* that "separate educational facilities [for black and white students] are inherently unequal," thus helping to pave the way for an end to segregation.

It should be added that the fifties ought not be judged unsparingly solely because they failed to eliminate every last vestige of racial discrimination. This is especially true when one considers black life in the fifties in full. In the wake of the success of the civil rights movement, it is only fair to ask whether or not anything good has been lost. Black Americans interviewed for the video on life in Chicago in the 1940s and 1950s were as one in saying that they missed those years, and not merely because they were young. The black family had not been destroyed. The percentage of illegitimate births among blacks was far lower. Crime rates in black America were lower. With far more reason to be bitter, most black folk during that time resisted the temptation to nurse grievances.

Almost all of them Christian, socially conservative, and patriotic, they lived their lives with dignity and hoped for a better day. Of Bronzeville, a black community on Chicago's South Side,

John Stroger, the first black president of the Cook County Board of Commissioners, said: "People [in the forties and fifties] took a great deal of pride in just being where they were. [Bronzeville] was economically poor, but spiritually and socially rich. People had hope that things would be better." As Alan Ehrenhalt has astutely observed, "it was a community all but frozen in place; but it was a community." The loss of that community is no small matter.

Another of the criticisms endlessly hurled at the 1950s is that it was an age of conformity, one that produced a "silent"—a politically apathetic—generation. In 1952 and again in 1956, so the narrative goes, Americans chose Ike, a bumbling figure who did nothing to upset the status quo, to be the country's president. They could and should have picked Adlai Stevenson of Illinois. Worse, with the commander (and golfer) in chief, they also elected Richard Nixon, discredited because of his role in the Alger Hiss case. This was unforgivable. Where was the radical spirit, the passion to change society? True, there were rebels like the Beats and the Columbia University sociologist C. Wright Mills, but they failed to arouse a sleeping population.

This is the view of the 1950s propagated by David Halberstam and other worshipers of the 1960s. What it really means, Joseph Epstein has written, "is that the 50s were not a good time for left-wing politics." It was not a time obsessed with politics, as all leftist eras are. Samuel Johnson once said of the politician George Lyttelton that "politics did not so much engage him as to withhold his thoughts from things of more importance." Those of us who came of age in the 1950s did not invariably turn our thoughts to the permanent things, but our lives did not revolve around the world of politics and social protest. We did not look to the federal government to cure our every ill or to protect us from our own folly. We wanted to be free—that is, morally responsible—beings.

We knew, of course, about the Cold War. But the claim, often advanced, that it left psychological scars on us is untrue. At no time did I or any of my friends toss and turn at night for fear of a nuclear attack. We worried about making a team or attracting the attention of a pretty girl. We were not forced to learn about "safe sex" and homosexuality in the second grade or about how our parents' generation was destroying the planet or about the many varieties of narcotics. We were allowed to be young, *and hence* we did not seek to remain young forever. We looked forward to growing up, to becoming adults. This was more important to us than what was going on in Washington, much less how we were going to change the world or "make a difference." To deplore all this is to bow before the will of those who tell us that the sixties, a time that has left mountains of human wreckage in its wake, constituted the greatest period in American history.

Remembering the fifties is not an exercise in nostalgia; it is an effort to take stock of what America once was and what it has now become. It is an opportunity to stop for a moment to reflect upon what has been gained and what has been lost. One of our greatest losses is of historical memory itself; without that memory a nation can never achieve self-knowledge. Nor can it make thoughtful decisions concerning the direction of its future and the future of its children. It simply moves ahead blindly, without bothering to count the costs of change, without asking not only whether something can be done but whether it *ought* to be done.

That is why, in addition to the pleasure it gives, remembering baseball in the fifties is so instructive. It brings into bold relief the decline represented by the contemporary game—with its drug scandals, multimillion-dollar contracts, designated hitters, multiplying franchises, hideous ballparks, and prohibitively-priced tickets. Fascination with the older game cannot easily be divorced from a growing recognition on the part of at least some Americans that history does not move in an ever-ascending direction.

Memory Skeptics

IN THE LAST QUARTER CENTURY, HISTORIANS HAVE FOCUSED A GREAT deal of attention on memory. In an endless stream, books appear on such subjects as the Great War and memory, the Holocaust and memory, slavery and memory. And they represent the tip of the iceberg. Revisionist studies of the past rooted in a suspicion of memory continue to flow from academic presses. Indiana University has established a Center for the Study of History and Memory in order "to address the growing interdisciplinary field of memory studies." The journal *History & Memory* "welcomes both case studies and theoretical contributions which question notions of memory, both lay and scholarly, and experiment with new methodologies for exploring its workings." The editors declare that they wish to explore "the manifold ways in which the past shapes the present and is shaped by present perceptions."

One of the principal presuppositions of this "turn to memory" is that present sociopolitical interests and power relationships determine not only what is remembered but *how* it is remembered. The "past," memory skeptics say, has been presented in such a way as to defend and advance the interests of those who control society. Geoffrey Cubitt, a knowledgeable student of the "turn to memory," cites a study in which Marcus Funck (York University) and Stephan Malinowski (Freiburg Institute for Advanced Studies) analyze the "masterful creation, selection and deployment of memory" by the German aristocracy. According to the authors, German aristocrats exploited autobiographical writing so as "to establish the image of aristocrats as natural leaders of society and vigorous opponents of the democratic rabble."

According to most "memory" historians, the flip side of the enlistment of memory in the service of power groups—the rich, the well connected, men—is the deliberate "forgetting" of certain events and peoples, the attempt to hide past injustices and to deny history's victims their rightful place in stories (I choose this word carefully) of the past. In this regard, Cubitt points to Yale Professor David Blight's claim, advanced in *Race and Reunion: The Civil War in American Memory*, that a portrayal of the American Civil War as a tragic but ennobling drama is nothing more than an attempt "to perpetuate racial injustice by denying experiences and memories of slavery and emancipation their crucial place in the nation's history."

For Blight and those like him, one of the primary tasks of the historian is to unmask and remedy such injustices. And that would merely serve as a beginning. The ultimate aims would be to advance the interests of those previously discriminated against and to reconstruct the social order in a more just—that is, a more egalitarian—fashion. The underlying assumption of all this is that historical knowledge, reliable knowledge of what occurred in the past, cannot, in principle, be attained. In the spirit of so-called "postmodernism," we are to understand that *nothing* can be known with anything like certainty. "Reality" is simply an interpretation of a particular observer; everything is relative to that observer's sociopolitical interests and prejudices. That being the case, it is perfectly legitimate, indeed obligatory, to promote a "reality" that elevates historical victims and leads to an egalitarian society.

Now the problem with postmodern (as with all) relativism is the obvious one: the statement that everything is relative must itself be relative. It cannot be *true* because that would mean that not everything is relative. Of greater concern, however, is the claim that, knowledge of the past being wholly unavailable to us, we are entitled to make it up, rather like a novelist—in accord (though this is left unspoken) with our political preferences. That is what "memory" historians insist most of their predecessors

120

have done—hence they are perfectly free to do likewise, but with purer motives.

As long as we are going to suspect history and memory, I should like to raise the suspicion that the "turn to memory" has as its aim that of which George Orwell warned: "Who controls the past controls the future: who controls the present controls the past." The words are from *Nineteen Eighty-Four*, in which the "Party"—modeled after the Communist Party of the Soviet Union—controls the past by rewriting it to suit its present needs, by dropping all evidence of the rewriting down "memory holes," and by scoring "an unending series of victories over [a person's] own memory." Or as Emmanuel Goldstein, the Party's arch-enemy, puts it: "The control of the past depends above all on the training of memory." Protagonist Winston Smith's problem is that he retains some memory of the past and knows that the Party regularly and systematically lies about it.

After Smith's arrest, Party leader and enforcer O'Brien tells him that "we, the Party, control all records, and we control all memories. Then we control the past, do we not?" But how, Smith cries, "can you stop people remembering things? It is involuntary. It is outside oneself. How can you control memory? You have not controlled mine!" In the end, readers of the novel know, the Party breaks Smith and gains absolute control of his memory. As Orwell understood so well, the ability to control memory posed a far greater threat than the control of action because it strikes at the heart of what it means to be human. "It is an inescapable fact about human existence," Edward S. Casey wrote in *Remembering*, "that we are made of our memories: *we are what we remember our-selves to be*." Memory control is the supreme ambition of totalitarians and those who possess totalitarian instincts. To frustrate that ambition, those who wish to be free must practice the art and discipline of remembering. Serious baseball fans do just that.

With Paul Ricoeur, I should like to warn "against the tendency of many authors to approach memory on the basis of its deficiencies, even its dysfunctions." No one denies that memory is imperfect, that it sometimes plays tricks on us. But it does not follow that nothing happened as we remember it. For one thing, there is often corroborating evidence, such as written records concerning the event in question. I think I remember the day in 1978 that my mother died, and when I consult her obituary I see that memory does not fail me. This may seem a minor matter but it is indicative of a larger truth, namely that we do not always have to rely upon unaided memory.

Nor are written records the only aid to memory. "One," Ricoeur wrote, "does not remember alone." A great many memories are in fact shared. We broaden and correct our memories by reminiscing with others. That is one reason why baseball and memory are so closely tied—baseball memories are widely shared by those who revere the game. "I love to be with people who have the same memories I have," New York Mets' fan Dana Brand has written, "people who share these things with me are not entirely strangers, even if I have never seen them before, even if I will never meet them."

All of us who were alive remember Bobby Thomson's home run. Even those who were not alive "remember" it because it is woven into the fabric of the game and of our national life; it has passed from generation to generation. Not only is the essential reliability of memory important to an individual's life, it is vital to our life together as a people. How else explain our efforts, for example, to record the memories of World War II veterans before they depart this life? The attempt, being pursued in some quarters with a vengeance, to discourage and cast suspicion on memory is a prelude to a further goal: to erase certain events and certain historical persons from our collective consciousness and replace them with lies and other persons, some of whom are unsavory. Baseball's continual invitation to communal remembrance can help us to avoid the fate reserved for those who forget.

Bibliography

*One of the principal sources for this book was my own memory, sometimes aided by that of others—and by reliable websites.

Books

Adomites, Paul, et al. *The Golden Age of Baseball*. Lincolnwood, Ill.: Publications International, 2003.

Ahrens, Art, and Gold, Eddie. *The Cubs: The Complete Record of Chicago Cubs Baseball*. New York: Macmillan, 1986.

Algren, Nelson. *Chicago: City on the Make*. Garden City, N.Y.: Doubleday, 1951.

——. *The Last Carousel*. New York: G. P. Putnam's Sons, 1973.

Alvarez, Mark, et al. *The Ol' Ball Game: A Collection of Baseball Characters and Moments Worth Remembering*. New York: Barnes & Noble Books, 1993 [1990].

Angell, Roger. *Game Time: A Baseball Companion*. Edited by Steve Kettmann. Orlando: A Harvest Book, 2003.

——. *Once More Around the Park: A Baseball Reader*. New York: Ballantine Books, 1991.

Aron, Paul. *Did Babe Ruth Call His Shot? And Other Unsolved Mysteries of Baseball*. Hoboken, N.J.: John Wiley & Sons, 2005.

Benny, Jack, and Benny, Joan. *Sunday Nights at Seven: The Jack Benny Story*. New York: Warner Books, 1990.

Billington, Charles N. *Wrigley Field's Last World Series: The Wartime Chicago Cubs and the Pennant of 1945*. Chicago: Lake Claremont Press, 2005.

Bloom, Ken. *The American Songbook: The Singers, the Songwriters, and the Songs*. New York: Black Dog & Leventhal, 2005.

Booth, Robert. *The Perfect Pafko: A Novel*. Seattle: Bugle Books, 2005.

Borer, Michael Ian. *Faithful to Fenway: Believing in Boston, Baseball, and America's Most Beloved Ballpark*. New York: New York University Press, 2008.

Brosnan, Jim. *The Long Season*. New York: Penguin Books, 1983 [1960].

———. *Pennant Race*. New York: Penguin Books, 1983 [1962].

Brown, Warren. *The Chicago Cubs*. Carbondale: Southern Illinois University Press, 2001 [1946].

Bryant, Howard. *Juicing the Game: Drugs, Power, and the Fight for the Soul of Major League Baseball*. New York: Plume, 2006.

Camerik, Howard. *The Curse of Carl Mays: A Novel*. College Station, Tex.: Virtualbookworm.com Publishing, 2006.

Canseco, Jose. *Juiced: Wild Times, Rampant 'Roids, Smash Hits, and How Baseball Got Big*. New York: Harper, 2005.

Carter, Paul A. *Another Part of the Fifties*. New York: Columbia University Press, 1983.

Casey, Edward S. *Remembering: A Phenomenological Study*. Bloomington: Indiana University Press, 1987.

Chambers, Whittaker. *Witness*. New York: Random House, 1952.

Conlan, Jocko, and Creamer, Robert. *Jocko*. Philadelphia: J. B. Lippincott, 1967.

Creamer, Robert W. *Baseball in '41: A Celebration of the Best Baseball Season Ever—in the Year America Went to War*. New York:

Penguin Books, 1991.

Cubitt, Geoffrey. *History and Memory*. Manchester: Manchester University Press, 2007.

Dawidoff, Nicholas, ed. *Baseball: A Literary Anthology*. New York: The Library of America, 2002.

DeLillo, Don. *Pafko at the Wall: A Novella*. New York: Scribner, 1997.

———. *Underworld*. New York: Scribner, 1997.

Dickey, Glenn. *The Great No-Hitters*. Radnor, Pa.: Chilton, 1976.

Ehrenhalt, Alan. *The Lost City: The Forgotten Virtues of Community in America*. New York: Basic Books, 1995.

Epstein, Joseph. *Fred Astaire*. New Haven: Yale University Press, 2008.

Erskine, Carl. *Carl Erskine's Tales from the Dodger Dugout: Extra Innings*. n. p.: Sports Publishing, 2004.

Fainaru-Wada, Mark, and Williams, Lance. *Game of Shadows: Barry Bonds, BALCO, and the Steroids Scandal That Rocked Professional Sports*. New York: Gotham Books, 2007.

Frommer, Harvey. *Five O'Clock Lightning: Babe Ruth, Lou Gehrig, and the Greatest Team in Baseball, the 1927 New York Yankees*. Hoboken, N.J.: John Wiley & Sons, 2008.

Fulk, David, and Riley, Dan, eds. *The Cubs Reader*. Boston: Houghton Mifflin, 1991.

Gelven, Michael. *Why Me? A Philosophical Inquiry Into Fate*. DeKalb: Northern Illinois University Press, 1991.

Gentile, Derek. *The Complete Chicago Cubs: The Total Encyclopedia of the Team*. New York: Black Dog & Leventhal, 2002.

Giamatti, A. Bartlett. *A Great and Glorious Game: Baseball Writings*. Edited by Kenneth S. Robson. Chapel Hill, N.C.: Algonquin

Books, 1998.

Gillette, Gary, and Enders, Eric. *Big League Ballparks: The Complete Illustrated History*. With Stuart Shea and Matthew Silverman. New York: Metro Books, 2009.

Golenbock, Peter. *Wrigleyville: A Magical History Tour of the Chicago Cubs*. New York: St. Martin's Press, 1996.

Goodwin, Doris Kearns. *Wait Till Next Year: A Memoir*. New York: Simon & Schuster Paperbacks, 1997.

Halberstam, David. *The Fifties*. New York: Fawcett Books (Random House), 1993.

———. *October 1964*. New York: Villard Books, 1994.

———. *Summer of '49*. New York: William Morrow, 1989.

———. *The Teammates: A Portrait of a Friendship*. New York: Hyperion, 2003.

Hemingway, Ernest. *The Old Man and the Sea*. New York: Charles Scribner's Sons, 1953.

Kahn, Roger. *Beyond the Boys of Summer: The Very Best of Roger Kahn*. Edited by Rob Miraldi. New York: McGraw-Hill, 2005.

———. *The Boys of Summer*. New York: Harper & Row, 1972.

———. *The Era, 1947–1957: When the Yankees, the Giants, and the Dodgers Ruled the World*. New York: Ticknor & Fields, 1993.

———. *The Head Game: Baseball Seen From the Pitcher's Mound*. San Diego: Harcourt, 2001.

Kinsella, W. P. *Shoeless Joe: A Novel*. Boston: Mariner, 1999 [1982].

Kundera, Milan. *The Book of Laughter and Forgetting*. Translated by Michael Henry Heim. New York: Penguin Books, 1981.

Larsen, Don. *The Perfect Yankee: The Incredible Story of the Greatest Miracle in Baseball History*. With Mark Shaw. Champaign, IL:

Sports Publishing, 2006 [1996].

Leavy, Jane. *Sandy Koufax: A Lefty's Legacy*. New York: Perennial, 2003.

Levine, Alan J. *"Bad Old Days": The Myth of the 1950s*. New Brunswick, NJ: Transaction Publishers, 2008.

Malamud, Bernard. *The Natural*. New York: The Noonday Press, 1952.

Moore, Joseph Thomas. *Pride Against Prejudice: The Biography of Larry Doby*. New York: Praeger, 1988.

Murphy, Cait. *Crazy '08: How a Cast of Cranks, Rogues, Boneheads, and Magnates Created the Greatest Year in Baseball History*. New York: Collins, 2008.

Muskat, Carrie, ed. *Banks to Sandberg to Grace: Decades of Love and Frustration with the Chicago Cubs*. New York: Contemporary Books, 2002.

Nemec, David, and Wisnia, Saul. *100 Years of Major League Baseball: American and National Leagues 1901–2000*. Lincolnwood, Ill.: Publications International, 2000.

Newhart, Bob. *I Shouldn't Even Be Doing This! And Other Things That Strike Me As Funny*. New York: Hyperion, 2006.

Oliphant, Thomas. *Praying for Gil Hodges: A Memoir of the 1955 World Series and One Family's Love of the Brooklyn Dodgers*. New York: Thomas Dunne Books, 2005.

Orwell, George. *1984*. New York: Signet Classics, 1950.

Paper, Lew. *Perfect: Don Larsen's Miraculous World Series Game and the Men Who Made It Happen*. New York: New American Library, 2009.

Posnanski, Joe. *The Soul of Baseball: A Road Trip through Buck O'Neil's America*. New York: William Morrow, 2007.

Pouletich, William. *Milwaukee Braves: Heroes and Heartbreak*. Madison: Wisconsin Historical Society Press, 2009.

Prager, Joshua. *The Echoing Green: The Untold Story of Bobby Thomson, Ralph Branca and the Shot Heard Round the World*. New York: Pantheon Books, 2006.

Reagan, Ronald. *An American Life*. New York: Simon and Schuster, 1990.

Rice, Grantland. *The Tumult and the Shouting: My Life in Sport*. New York: A. S. Barnes, 1954.

Ricoeur, Paul. *Memory, History, Forgetting*. Translated by Kathleen Blamey and David Pellauer. Chicago: The University of Chicago Press, 2004.

Robinson, Ray. *Matty: An American Hero: Christy Mathewson of the New York Giants*. New York: Oxford University Press, 1993.

Seidel, Michael. *Streak: Joe DiMaggio and the Summer of '41*. New York: Penguin Books, 1988.

Shaughnessy, Dan. *The Curse of the Bambino*. New York: Penguin Books, 2004.

Shea, Stuart. *Wrigley Field: The Unauthorized Biography*. With George Castle. Washington, D.C.: Potomac Books, 2004.

Sheed, Wilfrid. *Baseball and Lesser Sports*. New York: HarperCollins, 1991.

——. *The House That George Built: With a Little Help from Irving, Cole, and a Crew of About Fifty*. New York: Random House, 2008.

Silverman, Jeff, ed. *The Greatest Baseball Stories Ever Told*. Guilford, Conn.: The Lyons Press, 2001.

Snyder, Brad. *A Well-Paid Slave: Curt Flood's Fight for Free Agency in Professional Sports*. New York: Plume, 2007.

Sowell, Mike. *One Pitch Away: The Players' Stories of the 1986 League Championships and World Series*. New York: Macmillan, 1995.

———. *The Pitch That Killed: The Story of Carl Mays, Ray Chapman, and the Pennant Race of 1920.* Chicago: Ivan R. Dee, 1989.

Stromberg, Roland N. *After Everything: Western Intellectual History Since 1945.* New York: St. Martin's Press, 1975.

Theodore, John. *Baseball's Natural: The Story of Eddie Waitkus.* Carbondale: Southern Illinois University Press, 2002.

Tunis, John R. *Highpockets.* New York: William Morrow, 1948.

———. *The Kid Comes Back.* New York: Beech Tree, 1993 [1946].

Turner, Frederick. *When the Boys Came Back: Baseball and 1946.* New York: Henry Holt, 1996.

Vincent, Fay. *We Would Have Played For Nothing: Baseball Stars of the 1950s and 1960s Talk About the Game They Loved.* New York: Simon & Schuster Paperbacks, 2008.

Wallop, Douglass. *The Year the Yankees Lost the Pennant.* New York: W. W. Norton, 1954.

Ward, Geoffrey C. *Baseball: An Illustrated History.* New York: Alfred A. Knopf, 1994.

Warren, Robert Penn. *Democracy & Poetry.* Cambridge: Harvard University Press, 1975.

White, G. Edward. *Creating the National Pastime: Baseball Transforms Itself, 1903–1953.* Princeton: Princeton University Press, 1996.

Will, George F. *Bunts: Curt Flood, Camden Yards, Pete Rose and Other Reflections on Baseball.* New York: Scribner, 1998.

———. *Men at Work: The Craft of Baseball.* New York: Macmillan, 1990.

Wisnia, Saul. *The Wit & Wisdom of Baseball.* With Dan Schlossberg. Lincolnwood, IL: Publications International, 2007.

Zminda, Don, et al, eds. *Go-Go to Glory: The 1959 Chicago White Sox.* Skokie, IL: ACTA Publications, 2009.

Articles

Barra, Allen. "A Far-From-Instant Replay For Larsen, Berra and Fans." *Wall Street Journal*, February 27, 2007, p. D5.

——. "How Baseball Has Changed in 50 Years." http://online.wsj.com/article/SB123914799247399059.htm. Accessed April 11, 2009.

Barzun, Jacques. "On Baseball." In *A Jacques Barzun Reader: Selections from His Works*. Edited by Michael Murray. New York: HarperCollins, 2002, pp. 437–42.

"Baseball's Steroid Era." http://www.baseballssteroidera.com. Accessed May, 9, 2009.

Chen, Albert. "The Greatest Game Ever Pitched." *Sports Illustrated* 110, 22 (2009): 63–67.

Congdon, Lee. "Nostalgia and Historical Memory." *World & I*, 3, 8 (1988): 418–23.

——. "Permanent Things." *World & I*, 17, 6 (2002): 241–45.

——. "*Summer of '49*. By David Halberstam." *Continuity*, no. 14 (1990): 136–38.

——. "The Alchemy of Time." *World & I*, 12, 12 (1997): 249–55.

——. "*Ty Cobb*. By Charles C. Alexander." *Continuity*, no. 11 (1987): 98–100.

Editors. "Speaking Up for the Fifties." *New Criterion*, June (2008): 1. http://www.newcriterion.com/articles.cfn/Speaking-up-for-the-fifties-3852. Accessed June 5, 2008.

Eliot, T. S. "Tradition and the Individual Talent." In *The American Tradition in Literature*, II. Third Edition. Edited by Sculley Bradley, et al. New York: W. W. Norton, 1967, pp. 1269–76.

Epstein, Joseph. "A Boy's Own Author." In *Partial Payments: Es-*

says on Writers and Their Lives. New York: W. W. Norton, 1989, pp. 411–29.

——. "My 1950's." *Commentary*, September (1993): 37–42.

——. "Reflections: A Few Kind Words for Losing." http://us-info.state.gov/journals/itsv/1203/ijse/epstein.htm. Accessed June 29, 2008.

Goldstein, Richard. "Herb Score, 75, Indians Pitcher Derailed by Line Drive, Dies." http://www.nytimes.com/2008/11/12/sports/baseball/12score.html. Accessed August 26, 2009.

Kimmelman, Michael. "At the Bad New Ballparks." *New York Review of Books*, 56, 18 (2009): 22–23.

Leavy, Jane. "Chuck Stobbs, 1929–2008." *Washington Post Magazine*, January 4, 2009, pp. 15–16.

Petrocelli, Rico. "Tragedy and Tony C." http://www.bostonspastime.com/tonycbeaning.html. Accessed September 5, 2009.

Posnanski, Joe. "Where Are They Now? Stan Musial." *Sports Illustrated*, August 2, 2010, pp. 48–54.

Salter, Jim. "Honoring Career of Baseball's Carl Mays, Man Who Delivered a Fatal Pitch." http://www.cantonrep.com/lifestyle/history/x1528795964/Honoring-career-of-baseballs-Ca.... Accessed August 31, 2009.

Shapiro, Michael. "Of Heroes and Humans: Jim Brosnan Wrote About Himself, and Sports Writing Evolved." http://www.cjr.org/second_read/of_heroes_and_humans.php?page=all&print=true. Accessed October 25, 2009.

Verducci, Tom. "The Night the Lights Went Out in Mannywood." *Sports Illustrated*, 110, 20 (2009): 34–37.

Yardley, Jonathan. "A Deal With the Devil That Still Pays Dividends." http://www.washingtonpost.com/wp-dyn/content/article/2005/08/10/AR2005081002033. Accessed September 23, 2009.

Videos

Burns, Ken. *Baseball: A Film*. Florentine Films, 1994.

Remembering Chicago Again. WTTW Channel 11, Chicago, 1995.

DVDs

Damn Yankees.

Radio Days.

Reverse of the Curse of the Bambino.

Oral Tape

Baseball's Best Memories: 1927 to 1969. New York: Worldwide Entertainment Marketing, 1991.

Index

133